*The Process For Protected Tomorrows®, Take a Candid Look™, Create the Future Map™, Filter the Legal Options™, Capture Potential Benefits™, Document the Wonder™, Begin the Transition™, Fund the Future™, and Review and Renew™ are trademarks of Ehlert Financial Group, Inc., 2007. All rights reserved. Used with permission. www.protectedtomorrows.com Tel. 847.522.8086

**The Donor Motivation Program™ is a trademark of Wealth Transfer Solutions, 2007. All rights reserved. Used with permission. info@dmp-thekey.com Tel. 888.243.5172

†The 90 Day Check-Up System™ is a trademark of Canal Publishing Co., Inc., 2007. All rights reserved. Used with permission. www.90daycheckup.com Tel. 800.285.4008

††The True Wealth Transformer™ is a trademark of Paramount Financial Services, Inc., 2007. All rights reserved. Used with permission. www.missedfortune.com Tel. 888.987.5665

†††The 401k Coach™ and The 401k Coach Program™ are trademarks of EFS, 2007. All rights reserved. Used with permission. www.the401kcoach.com Tel. 877.9FAMCFO

†The Quadrant Living Experience™, The Brower Quadrant™, The Location And Vision Experience™, The Empowered Wealth Solution™, The Empowered Wealth Design Team™, The Solution Empowerment™, The Empowered Family Retreat™, and The Perpetual Confidence Builder™ are trademarks of The Quadrant Living Experience, 2007. All rights reserved. Used with permission. www.empoweredwealth.com Tel. 801.397.3300

††The Automatic Millionaire™ is a trademark of FinishRich Inc., 2007. All rights reserved. Used with permission. www.finishrich.com

†††The Parent Care Solution™ and Parent Care Specialist™ are trademarks of The Big Idea Co., LLC, 2007. All rights reserved. Used with permission. www.parentcaresolution.com Tel. 704.814.9965

Printed in Toronto, Canada. May 2007. The Strategic Coach Inc., 33 Fraser Avenue, Suite 201, Toronto, Ontario, M6K 3J9.

This publication is meant to strengthen your common sense, not to substitute for it. It is also not a substitute for the advice of your doctor, lawyer, accountant, or any of your advisors, personal or professional.

Library and Archives Canada Cataloguing in Publication

Sullivan, Dan, 1944-

The advisor century : value creation in an entrepreneurial

society / Dan Sullivan.

ISBN 978-1-897239-10-0

1. Financial services industry. 2. Investment advisors.

3. Financial planners. I. Title.

HG179.5.S85 2007   332.6068   C2007-903246-X

The
Advisor
Century

The Advisor Century

contents

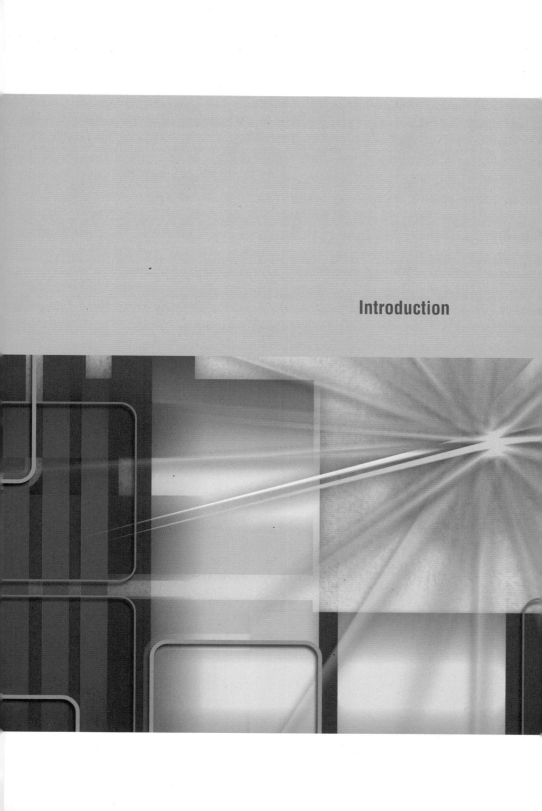

Introduction

The
Advisor
Century

Introduction

This entire book is organized around the following premise: *Never has there been a more exciting time to be a financial advisor.*

Let's look back to the year 1900. Just over a century ago, the concept of having a financial advisor was relatively foreign. Very few people had the privilege of having a personal advisor whom they could consult for financial wisdom. Such a service was more or less exclusive to royal households, leading politicians, powerful business magnates, and a few wealthy families. Indeed, I would go so far as to say that the idea of a financial advisor has been relatively foreign to most people for most of history. There simply wasn't a market for this kind of service, nor were there people equipped to provide it. The entire phenomenon that we call the financial services industry is a very recent event. I will argue in this book that it is a very crucial event for human progress everywhere on the planet during the 21st century.

During the years between 1900 and 2000, the financial services industry was essentially created from nothing. We saw the rapid development of an industry of financial professionals. This industry and its institutions became a mainstream part of everyday life for many people. Among other things, it facilitated the rapid growth of an "investor class" in developed countries. This was certainly an achievement. But the industry failed to realize its full potential. The 20th century represented Stage 1 of the industry's evolution. We are now ready for Stage 2.

Let's talk about the 21st century. Our argument is that the 21st century will eventually become known as "The Advisor Century." That's because no single group of professionals will be more important to the development of global society in the years 2000 to 2100 than financial advisors. No profession will be more influential. No profession will have more impact. No profession will be more useful. And no profession will do more to raise both our individual and collective capabilities.

Financial advisors will become the crucial "life-integrators" for millions of individuals, helping them transform their personal future and achieve a more fulfilling life.

They will also make enduring social contributions. Financial advisors will arrive at innovative social solutions in countless areas where government bureaucracies have failed. They will enable millions of people to become more productive "economic citizens," and to use their resources in a more socially empowering way.

As financial advisors make these contributions, they will also enjoy enormous personal rewards. While they will certainly acquire significant financial rewards, they will also achieve the entrepreneurial lifestyle and entrepreneurial freedom that many advisors currently desire, but do not have.

The 21st century and the advisors. I recognize that these are ambitious claims, and this is certainly an ambitious book. However, the reason this vision of the future we are advocating is so exciting is that *it is already starting to arrive.* In order to understand why this is The Advisor Century™, we must first understand the interplay between the "century" and the "advisor."

The century. *Millions of individuals are making "The Great Crossover" from economic childhood to economic adulthood.*

This "moment" in history that we are calling The Advisor Century represents the important confluence of certain social, economic, and technological trends. In an earlier book, *The Great Crossover®*, I explored many of these trends as they related to the crossover from an industrial world to one based on microtechnology. In this book, I will expand further.

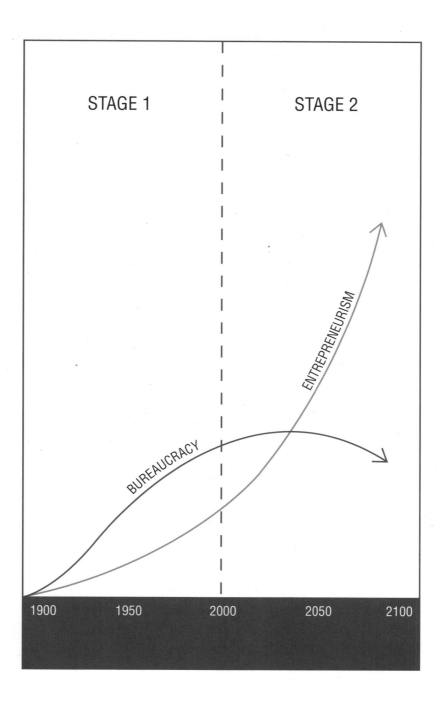

Our argument here is centered around several crucial points that describe the convergence of historical forces that will define The Advisor Century. Each one of these points is directly related to the impact of microtechnology on economic and social life. First of all, l argue that organizations in all fields are experiencing a crisis of confidence and capability. Microtechnology has provided countless opportunities to bypass these organizations in entrepreneurial ways. At the same time, individual consumers are experiencing unprecedented affluence.

- **From survival to transformation:** Because they no longer have to focus on fulfilling their daily survival needs, individuals are increasingly focused on their own "transformative" psychological needs.

- **Individuality and uniqueness:** People are focused on asserting their individuality and uniqueness in a world of choice.

- **Custom-designed consumption:** People want to experience personal growth and self-development, and they want consumption experiences that are attentive to these desires. For this reason, they are continually resistant to the commoditized offerings of large organizations.

- **Personalized attention:** People want personalized attention to their unique needs. And only entrepreneurs — empowered by microtechnology — can provide this attention.

The advisor. *Entrepreneurs with Unique Processes™ will transform client issues into myriad new forms of value creation.*

Our argument throughout this book will be that financial advisors are in the best position to capitalize on the forces associated with the microchip revolution. But only a certain kind of entrepreneurial advisor can make this impact. A select group of the most innovative financial advisors is already entering The Advisor Century. They are already making an tremendous impact, while enjoying extraordinary personal and professional rewards. Many of these advisors are in The Strategic Coach® Program. We call them Unique Process™

Advisors, and we will spend a significant portion of the book explaining just what it means to become a Unique Process Advisor. These advisors are at the vanguard of the industry, laying a path that others can follow. They share the following characteristics.

- **Client-focused:** Their chief interest, focus, and commitment is always with their clientele. As such, they consider the priorities and agendas of financial services companies as subordinate matters.

- **Process-based:** Their activities always take place within the framework of "Unique Processes," which provide their clientele with a greater sense of direction, confidence, and capability in a world of increased complexity.

- **Financially independent:** Their main source of income is the fees that clients and customers pay to go through their Unique Processes. These fees enable the Unique Process Advisors to eliminate their dependency on commodity-based compensation.

- **Have intellectual ownership:** In developing their Unique Processes, these advisors continually build a storehouse of legally-protected intellectual property that other advisors and the financial corporations are eager to license and use.

New financial industry. By looking at how this century is evolving and how the most advanced advisors are evolving within it, we can see the outlines of an entirely new financial services industry. On the following pages, we will specify what this new industry means for financial advisors. From our regular conversations with thousands of advisors, we believe that *The Advisor Century* will be a timely book. All of the changes we have described, which will be examined in greater detail throughout the book, are occurring at an accelerating rate. The opportunities are there to make fundamental changes, and so are the capabilities. What is lacking is a conceptual overview and a set of practical directions. In other words, a map and a gameplan. Here is what the map looks like:

We have decided to organize this book into three parts, each of which expands on a particular theme of The Advisor Century. Each part subsequently has several sections. We will argue that The Advisor Century is about three things: Opportunity, Freedom, and Usefulness.

The structure of the book.

1. Opportunity. The Advisor Century will provide entrepreneurial advisors with enormous opportunities. But they can only take advantage of these opportunities if they understand them. These opportunities exist because of changes that are occurring in the lives of individuals that affect financial consumers in particular ways. Throughout this book, we will focus on the transition millions of people are making from "economic childhood" to "economic adulthood." Financial advisors are in the best position of any professionals to help people make this transition. The opportunities available to advisors will be created because of this movement toward "economic adulthood." Specifically, they will occur in three areas:

- **Eliminating dependency:** Significantly greater numbers of people will seek to live their lives based on entrepreneurial principles and methods rather than bureaucratic ones. They will need entrepreneurial advisors to guide the way.

- **Relieving anxiety:** The 21st century will offer opportunities for large numbers of individuals to become affluent. Very few people have been educated and trained on how to take advantage of this. Entrepreneurial advisors will show millions of individuals how to overcome the anxieties that newly-created wealth brings with it.

- **Simplifying complexity:** A global society and economy governed by the evolution of microtechnology continually increases the daily complexity of work and life. The greatest problem of the 21st century, therefore, will be complexity. The most sought after solution will be simplicity.

Entrepreneurial advisors with Unique Processes will continually innovate concepts and tools that enable millions to simplify all aspects of their lives.

2. Freedom. In order for financial advisors to realize these opportunities and assist clients, they must themselves escape from the dependencies, complexities, and anxieties associated with industry "captivity." In this section, we will provide a focused strategy through which any captive advisor can achieve entrepreneurial freedom. Here, we will articulate what we call "the Unique Process path." We will demonstrate the steps necessary for becoming a Unique Process Advisor. They are as follows.

- **Creating intellectual property:** The key to entrepreneurial success in the 21st century is to create and own intellectual property. This consists of concepts, tools, and methods that produce transformative results. Financial advisors have traditionally sold the intellectual property created by corporations. Now they will produce their own within their Unique Process™ organizations.

- **Packaging client breakthroughs:** Using their intellectual property, Unique Process Advisors will continually innovate and package breakthroughs in all areas of clients' lives and work. These packaged breakthroughs will increasingly differentiate these advisors from all competition.

- **Achieving an experience monopoly:** Every Unique Process represents a unique market niche that is immune to competition and commoditization. Unique Process Advisors will continually expand their businesses and prosper by creating "experience monopolies" based on client breakthroughs that no one else can provide.

3. Usefulness. Entrepreneurial advisors will become some of the most useful people in the 21st century. They will do so in three ways:

- **Transforming client futures:** Millions of financial consumers are now looking for ways to transform their futures into ones with greater freedom, affluence, and significance. Every Unique Process provides some aspect of this transformation.

- **Transforming the industry:** Each Unique Process Advisor will provide innovations that many other advisors can use. Collectively, thousands of Unique Process Advisors will continually create the structure of an entirely new industry over the next hundred years.

- **Transforming society:** Over the past century, many improvements in society occurred through bureaucratic means. The world is now too complex and fast-changing for these rigid and unresponsive structures. Throughout the 21st century, many key social breakthroughs will occur as the result of innovations created by Unique Process Advisors. This is already beginning to happen.

Gameplan. We will conclude the book with a series of steps that advisors can take to get started on this path and enter The Advisor Century.

A personal note before beginning.

I remember the first time I became actively conscious of the financial services industry. It was in 1974 when I was working in my home city of Toronto. That was more than 30 years ago. At that time I was just beginning my coaching career, and I had very few of the insights that I have today — insights that have come after many years working closely with entrepreneurs and financial advisors from around the world. Yet even back in the 1970s, I found myself deeply interested in this profession. There was something unique and significant about financial advisors. There was something about the advisors I knew that distinguished them from other professionals in the marketplace and made them extraordinarily useful to their clients. I quickly came to a conclusion that I have held ever since: *If you want to be successful in this world, you'd better get yourself a financial advisor.*

My life has changed a lot since then. But what hasn't changed is my intense interest in the financial services industry, and especially the fate of its advisor-force. Through my organization, The Strategic Coach®, I've worked with thousands of entrepreneurs from dozens of different industries. I've given all of these entrepreneurs the same clear gameplan for achieving growth in both their personal and professional lives. I've given them the same set of principles, and preached the same set of habits. But over the years, I've found that my message resonates particularly well with financial advisors. Indeed, The Strategic Coach has more clients from the financial services industry than from any other industry — by a significant margin.

Motivated by freedom. For this reason, I've always had a particularly strong vantage point on the financial services industry. Every quarter, I meet with hundreds of financial advisors who constantly provide updates on their experiences in the industry. Over the years, I've come to observe that my financial advisor clients are extraordinarily gifted entrepreneurs. They have all the skills necessary to be successful, as well as a deep affinity for the entrepreneurial lifestyle. *Their primary motivation isn't status or money, but freedom: They continually desire increased control over their time, their relationships, their earning potential, and their daily activities.*

Constraints and burdens. Many of them entered financial services because they thought this industry could be a good springboard to the entrepreneurial lifestyle. They liked the fact that they could develop their own practice with a significant degree of autonomy, while also enjoying the support and infrastructure of a large financial services organization. Yet, over the years, many of these advisors have discovered an unpleasant fact. Huge segments of the financial services industry at the corporate level are anything but entrepreneurial. On a daily basis, financial advisors face new constraints and burdens from corporate managers, compliance officers, lawyers, and regulators whose agendas are to prevent advisors from doing anything innovative or entrepreneurial.

Many advisors that I talk to don't like this situation, but they also don't know how to create an alternative. For one thing, they are entirely dependent on the sale of commodity products for their livelihood. They have no independent revenue stream, and therefore no way to secure their livelihood outside of an organization's proprietary products. Yet as most advisors know all too well, commissions and fees have steadily declined, with no relief in sight. By all accounts, then, these are challenging times for many financial advisors. Over the past 15 years, I've observed countless frustrations among my own clients in the industry. These are some of the most successful advisors in the world, yet they have still felt under siege.

At one point, in the early 1990s, I actually spent several nights worrying about the future of my clients in the industry. It was at that point I decided to start developing a strategy by which advisors could escape from their organizational captivity and realize their ambitions as entrepreneurs. My efforts in this regard actually began in 1995 with the publication of *The 21st Century Agent*. In this book, I predicted that the "captive" agency system of the life insurance industry would continually disintegrate over the next 25 years. Much of what I predicted then has already come true.

Later, in *The Producer Group Future*™ (1998), I argued that the most powerful marketing organizations in financial services would be networks of independent advisors cooperating within "producer groups." Again, this has happened. Then, starting in 2003, The Strategic Coach began publishing the *Creative Destruction* subscription series. This product was centered on "12 Predictions" for the future of the financial services industry. I described the breakdown of bureaucratic structures and the emergence of an entirely new organizational form for financial advisors: the Unique Process.

What I have discovered over the past few years is that the predictions in all of these publications are coming to fruition sooner than anticipated. What has become clear to me is that we are entering a crucial moment in the history of this industry, characterized by a clash between two competing visions of what it means to be a financial advisor. We have reached a kind of tipping point. *Every financial advisor in the world today needs to understand the forces operating in the industry.* They need to understand why their life has become so difficult. But more importantly, they need to understand the enormous opportunities in front of them. And they need to understand how to get in a position to benefit from these opportunities.

Seeing the big picture ahead.

Ultimately, the overriding purpose of this book is to provide a new context through which thousands of financial advisors can think about both their daily working lives and their place in society. We are living in extraordinary times, ones that open up opportunities that have never existed before. It is in periods like this that entrepreneurs come to the fore. Again, I believe that the kind of financial advisors who develop Unique Processes are among the most creative entrepreneurs in the world. The time has come for financial advisors to develop an elevated conception of their profession. Too many financial advisors are so preoccupied with their daily frustrations that they can't see the big picture. Hopefully, by taking a journey into The Advisor Century, you'll become much more energized about the future of your profession. And you'll have both the confidence and the means to make that future a reality.

Dan Sullivan
Toronto, May 2007

1.
A Century Of Opportunity For Entrepreneurial Advisors

Part 1

The
Advisor
Century

Part 1:
A Century Of Opportunity For Entrepreneurial Advisors

For the past 30 years, I have been a coach to more than 6,000 financial advisors. My company, The Strategic Coach, works with advisors from virtually every financial services organization, with individuals coming from ten different countries. These advisors, because of who they are to start with, and because of the progress they have achieved over the years of working with us, are usually considered idea leaders and role models for thousands of other advisors throughout the industry.

Enthusiastic or pessimistic. From my experience, I have observed that financial advisors generally fall into one of two categories. Those who operate independently of large bureaucracies are increasingly optimistic and enthusiastic about their opportunities. Those, on the other hand, who are "captive" to bureaucratic organizations increasingly complain about restrictions, limitations, and obstacles placed in their way and are, therefore, pessimistic about things getting better in the years ahead.

Three understandings that make a crucial difference.
The 21st century will either be the most exciting of all times to be a financial advisor, or the scariest. Which it is depends on your knowledge, attitudes, skills, and habits. Above all, it depends upon on how you understand three things:

- **Your opportunity:** How the world is changing and what these changes are doing both to your existing and potential clientele.

- **Your freedom:** What your organizational arrangements are and how they impact your ability to act as an entrepreneur.

- **Your usefulness:** What you think your most important role is in identifying, meeting, and satisfying the changing requirements of clientele.

This book will be organized on the basis of these three understandings. Our fundamental thesis is that the 21st century offers unlimited opportunity, freedom, and usefulness for the right kind of financial advisor.

"Right kind" means those individuals who see themselves, first and foremost, as entrepreneurs, independent from the financial services bureaucracies that created and dominated the industry during the 20th century. Over the past 25 years, thousands of advisors have established independent relationships with these organizations, and many of the bureaucracies themselves have disappeared through mergers and acquisitions. Overall, there has been a dramatic decrease in the number of captive advisors in all sectors of the industry. Some have moved into different careers, while others have become salaried employees.

Product-focused versus client-focused. Among those advisors who have become independent, there are two categories: those who are primarily product-focused, and depend for their livelihood on the sale of commodities on a transactional basis to their clientele; and those who are entirely client-focused, using what we call the D.O.S.™ issues (dangers, opportunities, and strengths) of their clientele to create unique problem-solving processes.

The latter, whom we refer to as Unique Process Advisors, are paid primarily through upfront and ongoing fees for their value creation. They also receive commissions, but over time, their fee-based opportunities become so lucrative, multi-dimensional, and promising that they can afford to stop selling products altogether. Some even drop their licenses, achieving complete independence from all bureaucratic control.

At the present time, hundreds of advisors are approaching the marketplace with Unique Processes. They are enjoying remarkable success and virtually no competition. In the decades ahead, there will be tens of thousands more

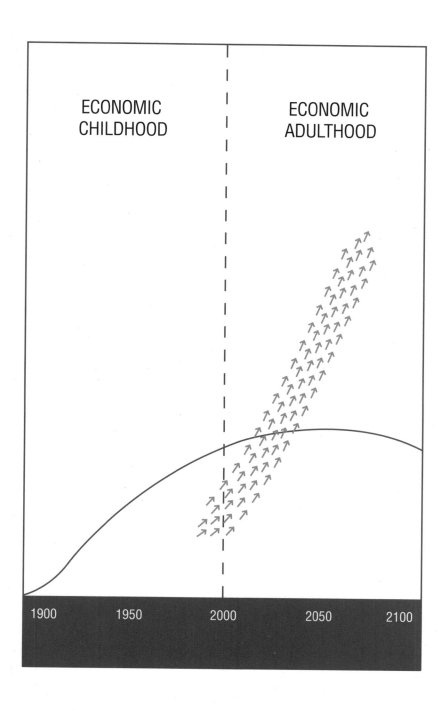

joining them. Over time, Unique Process Advisors will be seen not only as the industry's "thought leaders," but as cutting-edge innovators of new solutions for major social problems. That's because financial advisors are the only professionals who combine the disciplines of psychology and mathematics in their daily approach to client situations. Financial advisors — even captive and product-focused advisors — are in a better position than any other group of professionals to develop meaningful long-term relationships with clients.

Unique Process Advisors will experience increased opportunity, freedom, and usefulness in a world where their clientele experiences endless and unpredictable change.

In my work as a coach to financial advisors, I know literally hundreds of men and women who are geniuses at uncovering client needs and designing unique strategies to solve them. They have an uncanny ability to see life through other people's eyes, to walk through life in other people's shoes. This makes them extraordinarily clear and focused on creating and implementing unique solutions — a talent that improves as each of these advisors establishes and cultivates new client relationships.

With the best advisors, I have always had the feeling that I am dealing with psychological geniuses, who are also equipped with sophisticated financial knowledge, capabilities, and resources. Until recently, these great psychological abilities have been significantly underused, neglected, or suppressed because of the bureaucratic restrictions placed on their communications and activities.

Traditional bureaucratic controls weakening. Head office executives and managers over the past century have always focused on the mass distribution of commoditized products and services. This trend is unlikely to change because these bureaucrats are themselves generally incompetent in the area of client relationships. But with the increased turmoil taking place in financial organizations because of the globalization of financial services, the ability of bureaucratic leaders to control the activities of entrepreneurially-minded advisors is rapidly weakening. This is occurring for seven reasons:

- **Abandonment:** Large Industrial Age institutions are reneging on promises of lifetime employment and benefits to millions of workers, forcing them to provide for their own lifetime financial security.

- **Affluence:** The number of financial consumers who can pay for individualized treatment — and who reject commodity solutions — is increasing dramatically in advanced societies like the United States, Canada, the United Kingdom, and Australia.

- **Psychological self-determination:** Consumers increasingly want customized solutions and tools that are beyond the capability of bureaucratic organizations to comprehend and provide.

- **Crossover:** Advanced technological societies are rapidly "crossing over" from economies based on Industrial Age institutions to those dictated by the evolution of microchip-based tools and systems.

- **Computerization:** Hardware and software enable advisors to create sophisticated financial plans and solutions based on the best industry information, with no need to rely on head office capabilities or personnel.

- **The Internet:** Clients and customers can access information and seek out competitively priced products and services with little or no need for either company personnel or captive financial advisors.

- **Entrepreneurism:** Bureaucratic executives and workers in corporations, unions, and government are now being eclipsed in cultural prominence, social status, and economic power by individuals who create their opportunities through entrepreneurial activities and innovations.

Century-long shift of power. For most of the past century, financial advisors had to pay attention to the priorities and demands of financial corporations in order to get paid. Because of the seven factors listed above, this is no longer the case. Now financial advisors — especially those who have created Unique Processes — can establish completely independent lifetime financial relationships with their clientele.

A profound century-long shift of power is therefore taking place throughout the industry. Large financial corporations are increasingly disconnected from consumers who are looking to entrepreneurially-minded advisors for guidance, support, and solutions.

Simply put, with each passing day, more people in our transforming global society will be looking for financial direction and expertise because they are being forced to take control of their financial affairs and manage their own financial futures.

Fundamental change away from the industrial model.

This represents a fundamental change from the 20th century, when large organizations and institutions provided financial security for huge numbers of people. The Industrial Age was epitomized by Henry Ford, who recognized that mass production would only be possible if there was also mass consumption. In order to dominate the new automobile industry, he increased the salaries and free time of his workers, thereby giving them both the financial and leisure incentives needed to buy the very cars that they had helped to manufacture.

From that point forward, large corporations in all industries — along with growing unions and government organizations — appealed to workers through promises of lifetime employment and benefits. As the industrial economy grew, so did the number of executives, managers, and workers who were totally dependent upon large organizations for their livelihood and security.

The "good old days" lasted 25 years. In the United States, this institutional support became identified with "The American Dream," which promised a life of growing prosperity and satisfaction to those who worked hard and devoted their lives to employment within a single organization.

I grew up in the 1950s in northern Ohio, in the heart of the U.S. automobile and steel industries. When I graduated from high school, many young people in our area went to work in the car plants or in the mills. And what good jobs these were. By your mid-twenties, you had earned enough to buy a home and start a family. You could work for 45 years and have all of your financial matters taken care of by the corporation, by the union, or by the government. All your financial planning was done for you. If you needed a house loan or education for your children, it was provided by the corporation, as were your health and retirement benefits. Generous union contracts made these benefits possible.

Many people today think that this state of affairs lasted for a long time. In reality, however, the financial promise was only completely fulfilled during a 25-year period following the Second World War, when American corporations in all industries were on top of world markets. Rich labor contracts were possible because so much money was being made, and corporations felt confident promising lifetime employment and benefits to millions of workers. By the mid-1970s, the industrial economic model that supported this idyllic arrangement began to weaken and has now largely disintegrated. Five factors led to the end of these generous provisions:

- **Competition:** Most of America's economic competition had been flattened or set back by World War II. By the 1970s, these competitors re-entered the global marketplace, many of them with better, lower-priced products; more innovative production processes; and hungrier, lower-cost work forces. The U.K., Canada, and Australia faced a similar situation to America's.

- **Automation:** Microchip-based tools and systems replaced many manual-labor and routine office jobs with much more efficient machinery in all parts of the industrial economy, from the production lines to administrative departments.

- **Turmoil:** In the wake of the extraordinary costs of the Vietnam War,

President Nixon tried to protect the U.S. dollar by disconnecting it from the gold standard. This action introduced a period of unpredictable currency exchange turmoil throughout the world economy that caught financial officers of large corporations by surprise.

- **Inflation:** The oil shocks of the mid-1970s drove up the costs of energy throughout the industrialized economy, introducing a period of severe inflation that hobbled many large corporations and even destroyed some that were burdened with debts and unfunded liabilities.

- **Demographics:** The biggest generation in history, the American baby boomers, began entering the job market in large numbers just when the economy was stagnating and corporations were downsizing or disintegrating.

The beginning of economic adulthood. When the 1970s ended, the great Industrial Age was over, and with it the notion that large organizations could provide lifetime "cradle-to-grave" financial security. In a book I wrote in 1998, *The Producer Group Future*, I described this as the "end of economic childhood and the beginning of economic adulthood." This is a major evolution of society that I will return to many times throughout this book.

From this time on, individuals in America and other advanced countries would be required to take much greater responsibility for their own employment and financial security. There are still many backward-looking people who believe that things can be returned to the "good old days" of corporate welfare, but my contention is that none of the major forces of change in the world support this happening.

Everybody faces a new reality. This severe economic change means that a comforting and safe economic childhood is no longer possible for the majority of people in the world. It was not just the western industrial democracies that were forced to adjust to a new reality. As the 1980s began, the structures of Communist economies around the world started to fall apart, for the obvious reasons that they were hopelessly inefficient, grossly wasteful of human capabilities, and unable to produce anything of value that people were willing to purchase.

When the final collapse of Marxism as a belief system came in the early 1990s, more than 40 percent of the world's population was suddenly deprived of economic security. With far fewer resources, a bleak future, and no financial knowledge or skills, these workers in former Communist countries were cast out on their own. Many countries in the so-called Third World that had been bargaining for large amounts of foreign aid and making outright bribes during The Cold War, were also left without resources when the Soviet Union and its satellite empire collapsed. Countries in Africa, Asia, and South America that had relied on Soviet aid were left to fend for themselves economically for the first time — but with extremely modest skills and tools for doing so. And as wrenching as these changes were, they were just a taste of what was to come.

Endless global change becomes the new normal.

The Austrian economist Joseph Schumpeter coined the term "creative destruction" in the 1940s to describe the central dynamic of capitalism.[1] He identified the process of entrepreneurial innovation that was at the core of capitalist evolution as a never-ending destroyer of old structures and methods — and a creator of new ones. This destruction and creativity occurred in ways that were unpredictable, disruptive, and transformative. As insightful as he was, Schumpeter couldn't foresee how much the global process of creative destruction would be accelerated by the emergence of microtechnology in the 1970s.

Too complex to comprehend. Over the past 30 years, microchip-based tools and systems have been applied to countless situations in all sectors of the global economy. And not only the economy — microtechnology, as we grow to understand its virtually unlimited applications, is now seen as a crucial factor for progress in all areas of scientific, political, cultural, and social development. Simultaneously, all these diverse applications worldwide have been integrated into vast and myriad communication networks too complex to comprehend, culminating in what has now become the Internet, with its billions of daily uses and users.

We now live in a world where, every day, new opportunities for cooperation and competition emerge that were unimaginable 50 years ago. By the same token, we also live in a world where large numbers of people are faced with three serious dangers:

- **Confusion:** The experience of endless change driven by technology confuses people in many different ways. They lose their sense of where the center of things is, and they aren't clear on where to focus their thinking and actions. Because of this confusion about the present, they don't know how to invest their time, energies, and resources to produce a better future. *For many, it's more difficult to have a sense of personal meaning that keeps getting stronger. It's harder to have a sense of purpose that stays on track.*

- **Isolation:** Traditional forms of community based on mutually supportive relationships — extended families, small towns, neighborhoods, church membership, political parties, fraternal organizations, labor organizations, sports clubs — have weakened or disappeared from the lives of many people who live and work in modern settings. Even the most successful individuals often have few people they can confide in. There has been an increase in the number of temporary, transactional relationships in both personal and business spheres. *People feel less commitment to long-term relationships, and they sense the same in others.*

- **Powerlessness:** Conventional education is increasingly unable to prepare people confidently and competently for an unpredictable future. Knowledge and skills that were relevant five years ago can be worthless today. People who were successful in one setting find that changing circumstances are rendering them less useful and valuable. Specialists with 30 years of successful experience find that they have become redundant. *Many people find that they are falling farther behind in the constantly changing knowledge and methods that are crucial for success.*

I can remember going to Ohio in the late 1990s just as the newscasts were covering the closing of one of the last steel mills there. In newer mills around the world, much cheaper and higher quality steel was being produced by lower-cost workers using superior technology. A reporter was standing at the gates when the final shift came out. One worker, who was the fourth generation of his family who had worked at this site, looked particularly shocked and crestfallen:

"Why didn't they tell us this was coming? This is all I know how to do. What am I going to do now?"

The truth of the matter is that the mills had been shutting down for 25 years, and he had received hundreds of warnings from many different sources that this was likely to happen. It had been on TV, on the radio, and in the newspapers for decades. But everything that meant anything to this man — his extended family, his friends, his neighborhood, the bars where he drank, the alleys where he bowled, the church where all of his fellow workers and their families attended, and the one-industry town that had never changed — told him that everything was always going to be the same.

Now, suddenly, everything was going to be different in ways he couldn't comprehend. Nothing he had done up to that moment prepared him for what was to come. From this point forward, all the reassuring and protective communities he depended on would begin to fall apart, and quite quickly. He and his fellow steel workers would have to start life over again. Some, who managed to transform their lives and create better situations for their families, were eventually grateful for this disruption. For the majority of the workers, however, their future has never, and will never, be better than their past.

Creative destruction is the boss. This Ohio steel mill example is being repeated, not just in the old-line industrial sectors, but also within the most up-to-date fields of technology. White collars are treated the same as blue collars. Those with graduate degrees can lose as badly as those with no education at all. CEOs can be as disposable as temps. Global change is occurring not only in the most advanced countries, but also in societies still organized around hunting, herding, and agriculture. It's happening everywhere, all the time. And because of the unlimited usefulness of microtechnology — its endless users, applications, and by-products — the changes it causes are never going to stop evolving and accelerating. *That's the common experience for all six billion of us, now living together on a planet where "creative destruction" is the only permanent boss that hires and fires every individual.*

The "change disease" and us. In one way or another, then, to various degrees, in different situations, everyone on the planet now experiences these negative impacts of change. For some of us, they are a series of momentary situations that we successfully overcome and transform. For others, "the change disease" is like a low-grade fever that never goes away. These individuals are able to function, but there isn't much joy, energy, or optimism in their lives. Life is just one thing after another, and not much of it provides satisfaction or significance.

Individual and collective. For still others, the negative impacts of endless change are a worsening malady that undermines both their physical health and mental well-being. For them, the past has lost its comfort, the present offers no support, and the future has no meaning.

In many parts of the world, creative destruction affects people individually, with the impacts differing from one person to another. In other places, where traditional community structures are collapsing more rapidly — and where individuals are not skilled in personal self-transformation — there is a collective feeling of loss, dismay, foreboding, panic, and anger.

What I have just described is the bad news about the 21st century. The destructive side of creative destruction is never a pleasant experience. There's certainly a lot of destruction already making life scary, miserable, dangerous, and even deadly for millions of people everywhere. This will continue for the entire century. But the rest of this book will be about the good news caused by endless global change. It will be about the creative side of creative destruction. We will focus on the opportunities to be useful that entrepreneurially-minded financial advisors have in a world where creative destruction rules everything.

Let me briefly explain what kind of opportunities these are, because they are very different from the opportunities that financial advisors took advantage of in the 20th century.

Providing clients with a new sense of context that thrives on endless global change.

- **From products to transformations:** The opportunities of the 20th century were in expanding markets for selling products. The opportunities of the 21st century will be centered around addressing the expanding needs of clients for custom-designed transformations in their careers, communities, and lifestyles.

- **From quantity to quality:** The opportunities of the past century for advisors were in the increased quantity of sales they could achieve. The opportunities of the 21st century will be in the quality of creative growth partnerships they can develop with lifetime clientele.

- **From status to monopoly:** The opportunities of the past century were about gaining greater status, prestige, and perks within large financial corporations. The opportunities of the 21st century will be about forming continually evolving entrepreneurial enterprises that become market niche monopolies.

These three areas of opportunity reflect changes in the way people work and relate to one another in a world based on constant technological innovations and integrations. An entirely new set of needs has arisen from this technological revolution. These needs, in turn, require entirely different kinds of financial advisors.

In the following sections, I will examine three areas of emerging consumer needs that offer the greatest growth opportunities for those advisors who operate as independent entrepreneurs. As you can see from the brief descriptions that follow, these three areas all relate to the individual experience of adapting to technological change.

1. Eliminating dependency. *Moving away from bureaucratic dependencies in all areas of personal and work life.*

Increasing numbers of people are becoming aware that being connected to bureaucratic structures limits their ability to control their lives. Bureaucracies, by their very nature, lead to a loss of optimism, creativity, usefulness, and value wherever they influence people's lives. Escaping from bureaucratic dependency means adopting entrepreneurial attitudes and developing entrepreneurial capabilities. Financial advisors, therefore, will increasingly become the "freedom coaches" who enable millions of individuals to plan, make decisions, and take actions that lead to more liberated living based on entrepreneurial principles. *But financial advisors will only be able to do this if they have already liberated their own work and lives from bureaucratic control.*

2. Relieving anxiety. *Lifetime structures for living, working, and learning that take advantage of technological change.*

As our society transforms over time from industrial-based to microtechnology-based modes of production and organization, millions of individuals feel anxious about their livelihood and feel uncertain about the meaning of their lives. These anxieties are similar to what people felt when the last great transformation took us from an agricultural to an industrial society. Many new rules must be learned to become personally successful. Many new ways of investing time and effort must be mastered to produce satisfactory results in the future. Instead of drawing their confidence from the outside, individuals must learn how to create their confidence from their internal sense of personal capability.

Financial advisors who operate in an entrepreneurial fashion have already learned to produce their own confidence. They are uniquely positioned to help others do the same. *But this is only possible for those advisors who have freed themselves from commodity sales as their main source of income and are, instead, focused entirely on creating value for their clientele.*

3. Simplifying complexity. *Continual individual progress and growth in situations where others are blocked by obstacles, limitations, and restrictions.*

A technological world is far more complex and complicated than an industrial one, from both social and economic perspectives. Impersonal transactions based on automated processes proliferate, and personal service declines in both quality and availability. Even the wealthiest and most successful people feel increasingly frustrated by the inability to be efficient and productive.

Financial advisors, because they combine both mathematical and psychological skills, are able to provide a level of personalized, satisfying service unavailable from any other profession. *But only those financial advisors who have escaped from the regulatory complexity and complications of the financial services industry are capable of providing this kind of service on a dependable, long-term basis.*

Opportunities, freedom, and usefulness. The technological transformation based on the microchip is creating a completely new environment of opportunities for the right kind of financial advisors. In the following three sections, we will expand our description of the three opportunity areas listed above. In the rest of the book, we will explain how financial advisors can increase dramatically both their freedom within the financial services industry and their usefulness to their clientele.

Opportunity 1:
Eliminating Dependency

It's always much easier to change a technology, to change a way of getting work done, than it is to change the way people think and act. This is because it's much easier to change a mechanical system than to change what living, breathing human beings consider to be normal. Once people get used to one kind of "normal" in their lives, it's very difficult and painful for them to accept another kind.

Over the past 30 years, the microchip in developed countries has dramatically altered the system of mass industrialization that once required large numbers of workers. The factories are just as massive, but they have very few people, because workers have been replaced by automated controls and processes. In Japan, for example, there are automobile factories that are operated almost entirely by robots. What this means is that large bureaucracies aren't needed anymore for large economic processes and results.

Everybody a dependent. Unfortunately, over the past hundred years, bureaucracy was the way everything was done. Bureaucracies were crucial to economies and societies in the 20th century because they were the only way we could organize complex activities and interactions among large populations. The bureaucratic model was adopted everywhere, not just in the economy, but also in government and education. Everything was done in a bureaucratic way. Most people thought about things in a bureaucratic fashion. And the great majority of people wanted to get ahead in life by securing employment in a bureaucracy. People were rewarded and promoted based solely on their mastery of bureaucratic processes and rules. Everybody and everything became bureaucratically dependent.

This society saw its climax during the years immediately following World War II. After all, the military is the world's most bureaucratic and hierarchical form of organization. And in many ways, the allied war effort displayed large organizations at their most productive and powerful. Everybody was mobilized around a single goal, and they knew that the collective power of large organizations was necessary to secure victory.

When young soldiers came back from war, they raced to secure a solid white-collar job in one of the huge corporate bureaucracies. They saw these jobs as the ticket to middle-class prosperity — a way to support a "suburban" lifestyle for their young families. As a result, large organizations acquired unprecedented social and cultural influence; the dominant cultural image of this age was thousands of men dressed in the same grey flannel suit, getting off a train and walking to their desk job at a corporate office. Writing in the 1950s, social critic William Whyte exposed this society of "the organization man." Whyte brought attention to those members of the middle class who had "left home, spiritually as well as physically, to take the vows of organization life."[2]

Starting in the 1960s, though, something began to change. The baby boom generation increasingly began to resist "the organization man" lifestyle. They wanted more opportunities to assert their individualism. The most extreme examples of this trend were the hippies and student radicals, but gradually this celebration of the "individual" became widespread — challenging the older culture of conformity.

The microchip revolution.

Then, something happened that nobody could have predicted. The advent of microchip technology in the 1970s totally revolutionized the social and economic landscape — weakening large organizations and elevating the "individual" as never before. People who grew up with bureaucratic attitudes and behavior have since been pressured to change the way they think and act — and the way they relate to one another.

That's because the microchip is not just another technology; it is the very essence of continual technological evolution.

Microchips creating microchips. Previous advances in technology were achieved by applying different technologies to each other to create something different. The microchip advances by being applied to itself. Existing microchips are used to create even more powerful new microchips. The speed and power of a microchip continually changes for the better, but it is always still a microchip. Each new generation makes possible an even more powerful generation — with no upper limit of usefulness. The greater our existing microchip capabilities, the greater our future capabilities will be. But from the first generation to the hundredth, we are always dealing with a microchip.

Nothing like this has ever happened in human affairs — the ability to endlessly expand productivity, cooperation, and creativity through the evolution of a single technological device.

From incremental to exponential. What this means is that sometime during the 1970s, human progress based on technology went from being incremental to being exponential. Before the microchip, progress on the planet proceeded by addition; after the microchip, it proceeds by multiplication. But not for everyone.

The vast majority of people in global society are still constrained within systems of slow growth or no growth. The developed world, led by the United States, is moving quickly from industrialization to microtechnology as the engine of economic growth. But many other countries are only now entering the Industrial Age, roughly where North American and Northern European societies were in the early 1900s.

China, India, Brazil, and the "Asian tigers" are examples of these emerging industrial societies. Still other countries and regions, many of them in the Middle East, Africa, and Latin America, remain largely pre-industrial. Looking at the complete spectrum of countries in the world, a vast disparity exists between those that are able to take advantage of microtechnology and those that don't even know where to begin. Therefore, within the global network of nations, there are "have" countries, and countries that are "have-nots." Since the haves are progressing at an exponential rate, these global disparities will only increase during the 21st century.

Same country, different century. What is true between nations is also true within them. In the U.S., for example, there is a growing number of individuals whose lives are firmly attached to microchip evolution, and there are still many who lack the attitudes and skills to work within even a 20th-century industrial framework. One of the analyses of the civic breakdown following Hurricane Katrina revealed that in some New Orleans families, no one had worked for three generations. They lacked the knowledge, attitudes, skills, and habits to do even the most basic industrial work. In terms of The Great Crossover from an industrial to a microchip-based economy, these men and women are not simply economic children — they are economic infants. They are living in the same country but not in the same century. They may live only five miles from the "haves," but for all practical purposes, they are separated by more than a hundred years of technological progress.

On top, but going down. At the same time, there are other individuals in rich countries who became wealthy during the Industrial Age — but whose fortunes are now waning. Their pasts are much bigger than their futures. They may still be in positions of power, status, and influence, but the clock of technological change is ticking against them. They had all the capabilities to be successful in the 20th century, but not in the 21st. They went to the right schools, joined the right corporations and organizations, were invited to the right clubs, and had the right friends, but none of this makes them "Microchip Friendly." They may know the words of technological progress, but they don't know the tune. They have always been on top from a bureaucratic standpoint, but not an entrepreneurial one. Their way of working and living is based on old ideas and methods. Although by all outward appearances they seem to be "haves," their prospects are sliding backward.

The New York Times periodically features stories about senior executives laid off from prestigious corporations, who have been out of work for more than five years. They are angry and bewildered that their credentials and connections are not creating any new opportunities. By all external criteria, these individuals, who often still live in affluent neighborhoods, should be counted among the "haves." But their attitudes and capabilities are steadily relegating them to the ranks of the "have-nots." If their children follow their example, they will also become have-nots.

Learning and growth, not status. There is yet a third group of individuals to consider. This is the classic rags-to-riches story in the United States. It's classic because it occurs so frequently. These individuals were born into conditions that labeled them as "have-nots." But they refused to accept this condition and aspired to a better life. While their parents and other family members may be permanent have-nots, they are determined to progress further. They may have come from another country — often from a have-not society — with only their ambitions, but they steadily developed the attitudes and capabilities to make their dreams a reality. Since they want a bigger future, they bypass the past. Invariably, they choose a path supported by microtechnology.

They are drawn to everything that's new, better, and different — and ignore the old and accepted ways of doing things. They're not interested in status; they are motivated by learning and growth. As they progress, they overtake many individuals who were born with far more advantages.

I provide these three scenarios to point out that any discussion of 21st-century inequality between societies, and within societies, must be understood within the context of the evolution of microtechnology. People can blame other causes but they all come back to the constant increase of the microchip's speed, power, and usefulness. There are certainly many political, social, and cultural considerations involved in the disparity between haves and have-nots, but these are always subordinate to the technological forces. Those who understand and are able to utilize the microchip's advantages continually gain advantages of their own. Those who do not acquire this understanding are increasingly at a disadvantage.

There are endless things that can be written about the inequality being caused by the evolution of microtechnology — but I will leave this to other writers. My purpose in this book is to create a world view of the 21st century for those financial advisors who choose to be truly entrepreneurial in the marketplace. One of the most important things for these advisors to realize is that their number one job for the rest of their careers is helping everyone they meet become more of a "have" within global society. In other words, it means moving their clientele away from economic childhood and toward greater economic adulthood.

The tendencies and habits of 21st-century "haves."

Because being an economic adult is now geared directly to microchip evolution, staying in touch with what's required demands constant alertness, learning, adaptability, and improvement. For this to happen, advisors themselves must increasingly take on the qualities that I call "microchip wisdom." These are the tendencies and habits that characterize the "haves" in our technologically advanced society.

Self-responsible. Throughout the 20th century, most people depended on corporate and government employers to take care of them. In other words, someone else was responsible for creating their opportunity, their activities, and their security. In the 21st century, those who become self-responsible and take control of their economic lives — creating their own economic capabilities, opportunities, and security — will be the most prominent people in society.

Bureaucracy-free. Within bureaucracies in any sector — public or private — virtually everyone is an economic child. This is true of even the senior executives and managers. Without their bureaucratic jobs, they are bewildered and helpless. Becoming an economic adult in the 21st century requires people to remove themselves from bureaucratic restrictions and controls. It requires them to eliminate all bureaucratic attitudes, behaviors, and aspirations from their thinking.

Global teamwork. The vast majority of individuals think and operate only within national borders. In fact, many never operate outside of a local framework. Those who are successful in the 21st century will be comfortable and capable with global connections. Since their focus is on maximizing communication, cooperation, and creativity, they must have the option to go beyond national borders in search of the teamwork and alliances required for personal advancement.

Intellectual growth. The industrial model of the 20th century confined learning mostly to formal schooling and the early years of one's work career. After a certain amount of career success, daily life became about maintaining, preserving, and defending what you already had rather than growing intellectually. Anyone who thinks this way in the 21st century will very quickly lose out. What is required now is never-ending curiosity — taking on ever more difficult intellectual challenges. The 21st century is a brain century. Those who don't use their brains lose everything.

Self-transforming. Within industrial bureaucracies, personal progress is measured by increases in control and status. After a certain point, none of this has anything to do with skills or achievement. Being promoted beyond one's level of competence is a well-known bureaucratic phenomenon. Those who aspire to economic adulthood are focused on two things: increasing their capabilities and growing their ambitions. As they reach their current ambitions, they use this achievement to develop new capabilities, which makes possible even greater ambitions. In this way, upward progress becomes endless.

Like-minded community. For most of human history, our most important "community" was determined by family ties, geography, religion, politics, and particular economic activities. With the increased capabilities provided by microtechnology, individuals are forming many different kinds of communities to satisfy different personal interests and needs.

To give just one example, on the popular Internet site, Meetup.com, there are thousands of virtual communities for every conceivable hobby or interest, from dumpster diving to Scrabble, bee-keeping to capture the flag. These communities allow members to interact with people who share their interests and organize more formal face-to-face meetings. The most important community consists of like-minded individuals around the world who are striving in similar ways for economic adulthood.

Committed to creativity. The predominant values of industrial society were based on collective predictability, control, consistency, and security. These were excellent guidelines and goals for organizations and societies that experienced gradual, incremental changes. However, the microchip revolution turns everything on its head. During this century, the most important values will be individual learning, creativity, innovation, inventiveness, and enterprise — regardless of how these forces impact our collective values. In the 20th century, it was up to individuals to adjust to the collective; in the 21st century, the collective must adjust to individuals. The microchip makes this possible, it makes it paramount, and it makes it irreversible. Economic adulthood means always betting on individual capability and creativity over collective predictability and consistency. Those who are most successful will be committed to anything that increases human capability and creativity — anywhere in the world.

Maximum impact. The industrial model of the 20th century established one's working life from their early twenties to age sixty-five, after which individuals were "retired" — that is, taken out of use. If you were going to have any achievements, they would have to take place during this 40-year window. If you were going to make a major contribution, it had to occur before retirement. This entire mentality is fast disappearing in a microchip-based society. Individuals will increasingly experience their greatest career successes in their early eighties and nineties, and they will make significant contributions until the day they die. Economic adults never plan to retire from the process of learning, striving, achieving, and creating new value in the world. No one else limits or controls their capabilities and ambitions — and they keep increasing their contributions for as long as they live.

The 21st century "haves," then, are those who adopt these attitudes of "microchip wisdom" and put these principles to use in all areas of their life. In the process, they become the "wealthiest" people in society. Not only will they accumulate significant income and assets, their conception of "wealth" will extend well beyond those more traditional measures. What does it mean to be wealthy in a microchip society? Consider these rewards that people with "microchip wisdom" are experiencing:

- **Meaning:** They feel that they are at the forefront of economic, political, cultural, and social progress.

- **Purpose:** They feel that they are demonstrating through their activities and achievements how life can be for everyone else.

- **Capability:** They feel that the new tools and systems provided by micro-technology lead to ever increasing powers of creativity, productivity, and cooperation.

- **Opportunity:** They feel that things will always get bigger and better, and that their future is only limited by their imagination.

- **Independence:** They feel that they are in control of the forces and factors that make their future bigger and better.

- **Influence:** They feel that they are important people within their society — respected and admired.

- **Significance:** They feel that what they contribute to others is greater than what they receive — and that their success is justified by the value they create.

- **Health:** They feel that age is an attitude, and that being perpetually young is a function of being motivated, productive, and useful.

- **Enjoyment:** They feel that the contribution they make to society entitles them to the best that society offers in the way of luxury, entertainment, recreation, and learning.

- **Ease:** They feel that their personally-generated success entitles them to be supported and served by the best abilities of other people.

- **Income:** They feel that their ability to make money is constantly growing, and that the opportunities for doing so are always increasing.

- **Assets:** They feel that they will always have more money than they need, and that this surplus is a growing source of confidence, creativity, and capability.

The New Wealth.
The 12 rewards just outlined are extraordinary. Most people would find them highly desirable, and they are within reach for an increasing number within modern societies. Many entrepreneurially-minded people have already achieved these rewards, and many more are striving for them. In the years ahead, they will become the central pursuit for hundreds of millions. Taken as a whole, these 12 rewards constitute what I call "The New Wealth" of the 21st century. The Industrial Age had its concept of wealth, and the microchip age already has an entirely new and expanded concept.

The microchip revolution has greatly enhanced our capabilities and opportunities, and therefore has expanded our notion of what it means to be wealthy. This concept of wealth goes far beyond what was "normal" in the 20th century. The 12 rewards listed above far exceed what was possible for individuals to achieve or even imagine within industrial bureaucracies and the societies that grew up around them.

Organizing principle. This concept of New Wealth will now be used as a central organizing principle throughout the rest of the book. The New Wealth makes it possible for us to identify the opportunities for financial advisors in the decades ahead, and the areas where their freedom and usefulness lie.

The 21st-century transformation from economic childhood to economic adulthood.

One way of looking at the current period of history is that the entire human race is in a 50-year crash-course learning process, striving to master entirely new capabilities. Everybody on Earth is a willing or unwilling student in this school, and nobody can escape from the lessons that are being taught. Everyone is continually being tested and graded. Those who pass their tests are promoted, and those who fail are held back until they are willing and able to learn. This period of planetary schooling will span the years from 1975 to 2025, after which a critical mass of the global population will be comfortable and confident with the demands and possibilities of microtechnology. For me, "critical mass" would mean in excess of two billion individuals, worldwide, who are achieving personal daily success because of the advantages provided by microchip-based tools, systems, processes, and networks.

Microchip-Friendly people. By 2025, everyone who was in a position of control and influence in 1975 will be dead or retired from active life. Most of the bureaucratic mentality and methodology that still controlled society in the late 20th century will have disappeared. The bureaucratic leaders of 1975 will have been succeeded by individuals for whom operating in a microchip-based economy and society feels "normal." By that time, there will be hundreds of millions of Microchip-Friendly individuals who have achieved, or are capable of achieving, all 12 rewards of The New Wealth. Here is what I mean by "Microchip Friendly."

- **Daily use:** Your daily work and lifestyle make extensive use of personal computers and global digital networks.

- **Personal multiplier:** Your personal capabilities are continually multiplied, rather than undermined, by each new evolution of technology.

- **Collective capability:** Your personal success involves ever greater creativity, communication, and cooperation with increasing numbers of other Microchip-Friendly individuals.

- **Unique talents:** You are personally supported in all areas of work and life by networks of individuals with unique talents who also take advantage of microtechnology.

- **Increasing knowledge:** You enjoy direct access to greater amounts of personally useful knowledge in an expanding number of areas.

- **Supportive society:** You are in a society whose economic, political, cultural, and social progress is directly based on advances in microtechnology.

- **Asset growth:** Your financial assets are continually growing because of the greater applications of microtechnology in all areas of human activity and enterprise.

- **Belief system:** Your spiritual, philosophical, political, and social beliefs are based on a comfort with microtechnology. You believe microtechnology is a natural and beneficial expression of human progress, and you are confident it will keep getting better.

At present, Microchip-Friendly people, as described above, are a minority of the population. But their numbers are growing at an exponential rate. The extraordinary progress of just China and India over the past decade indicates how much greater global progress will be by 2025. The vast majority of human beings are under the age of thirty. They have little or no investment in the old society of industrial bureaucracies — and the evolution of the microchip is making it continually easier for them to access its benefits. Microchip wisdom will be easier for them to adopt. The New Wealth will be their personal lifetime goal from an early age, and they will be Microchip-Friendly from the very start of their education and training.

Economic adulthood. From what has been written so far, we can now piece together a useful description of what I call "economic adulthood" — as contrasted with the economic childhood that characterized work and life in the era of industrial bureaucracies.

Economic adults are those individuals whose attitudes and behavior are based on the attitudes of "microchip wisdom," who are enjoying the 12 rewards of The New Wealth, and who are "Microchip Friendly" in all areas of their work and life.

Economic children, on the other hand, are the billions of individuals who have not transformed themselves in these three evolutionary ways — or who are only in the early stages of doing this. By looking at all of society from this perspective, it simplifies our understanding of what is taking place right now in the world. It simplifies our predictions of what is going to take place over the next hundred years.

All of the major issues of the 21st century will have at their core the transformation of human society from economic childhood to economic adulthood.

Over the next hundred years, the most important scientific breakthroughs will be by-products of this transformation, as will the continued evolutions of technology. All economic life will reflect this transformation, as will political developments in every society. All cultural life will become an expression of this transformation. And all social relations in every place and situation will be manifested by the migration of billions of individuals from economic childhood to economic adulthood.

As a planetary society, then, from the years 2000 to 2100, we will be moving from being a large population with lives mostly based on bureaucratic dependency to being an even larger population with lives mostly based on entrepreneurial independence. The period between 1975 and 2025 — "The Great Crossover" — is the time frame during which the foundations of this transformation are being laid.

My belief is that the single most important industry involved in this Great Crossover is financial services. Financial advisors who aim to be uniquely useful in helping others make this transition and take on the characteristics of economic adulthood must be acquiring all of these characteristics for themselves.

The Transformation Agenda.
In light of this discussion, here is what billions of people in all parts of the world now need to successfully make the transition to economic adulthood.

- **Entrepreneurism:** An entrepreneurial philosophy of life based on practical concepts, processes, and tools.

- **"Wise" communities:** Access to communities of other individuals who are also following an entrepreneurial path to the future — individuals who think and act according to the principles of "microchip wisdom."

- **Escape from dependency:** Strategies for escaping from and avoiding bureaucratic dependency in all areas of their personal and professional life.

- **Everything "friendly":** Continual practical transformation of every aspect of their lives to be more Microchip-Friendly.

- **Shared benefit:** Assistance in helping their families and friends — all those who matter to them — make these transformations.

- **Growth economics:** Direction, expertise, and resources to transform local economies so that people can grow and prosper from the global microchip revolution.

Entrepreneurial financial advisors as the agents of creative change.

The list on the previous page constitutes what I call "The Transformation Agenda." It represents a lifetime growth opportunity for those financial advisors who are taking an entrepreneurial approach to their careers and their clientele. Financial advisors are and will increasingly become the global agents of creative change for billions of individuals seeking greater economic adulthood. Advisors will fill the voids left by employers and government to become the new support system. Yet while advisors provide support, they will never demand dependency. The relationship between financial advisors and their clients will always be about empowerment.

Within the The Transformation Agenda, there are countless opportunities for advisors to create new kinds of value in the marketplace. In The Strategic Coach community, there are hundreds of individuals who are successfully pioneering transformational processes that represent a dramatic departure from the way business is done in the financial bureaucracies that still dominate the industry.

These "Unique Processes" represent both the best vehicle for helping individuals to become economic adults and the best entrepreneurial structure for advisors to enjoy ever greater success, satisfaction, and significance. We will describe a number of these processes in Part 3, which focuses on how advisors can dramatically increase their usefulness in the 21st century.

Opportunity 1 in The Advisor Century.

This section of the book is called "Opportunity 1" because The Transformational Agenda represents our foremost opportunity for growth over the next hundred years. This escape from bureaucratic dependency involves all of humanity. Throughout the entire world, the microchip revolution will continue to provide greater capabilities and opportunities for individual independence. Entirely new structures and processes will be needed to accommodate our transition to greater economic adulthood. After coaching thousands of creative and intelligent financial advisors over the past 30 years, I'm certain that these advisors represent the ideal agents of change. Yet as they help people achieve success as economic adults, advisors will also be called upon to help clients deal with the new anxieties and complexities that independence creates. In the following section, Opportunity 2, I will examine how advisors can help millions of individuals deal effectively with the personal anxieties that are an unavoidable part of their passage to economic adulthood.

Opportunity 2:
Relieving Anxiety

One of my long-time Strategic Coach clients, a very successful financial advisor who works with wealthy business owners and their families, had this insight: *"Some of my wealthiest clients are the most anxious. They have way more money than they can possibly spend. They're really nice people, with everything going for them, and they seem to be worried about everything. Being well-off hasn't made them happy."*

This comment highlights an essential quality of life during the crossover from an industrial to a microchip-based economy and society. People have generally never been more affluent, or more anxious about it. The more it becomes possible for people to increase their incomes and assets, the less secure many of them feel about the technologically-driven world that is making this possible.

Affluence forces people to make difficult and painful decisions about how to allocate their resources in a world with ever more options. People often wonder what they have done to deserve the affluence that so many of their ancestors were never able to experience. They fear that the pressure to preserve and expand their material wealth is causing them to neglect their spiritual and emotional health.

I believe that this anxiety caused by increased affluence offers the second great opportunity for financial advisors to be extraordinarily useful throughout the 21st century. More than any other professional in the marketplace, financial advisors are called upon to help people come to terms with their affluence and use their affluence in an empowering way.

Put simply, the more anxiety there is, the more opportunity there is for entrepreneurial advisors to provide direction, confidence, and capability to tens of millions of individuals who are living in a society where many influential people are obsessed with bad news. *My contention here is that the anxieties most people have are tied to perceptions, not reality.* In spite of the many people who predict and expect things to get worse, the truth is that over the past 25 years, things have been getting better around the world. In many cases, remarkably so. For every anxiety that things might turn bad, there are many more opportunities for things to turn out well. Financial advisors who understand this and take advantage of positive global trends will be in a unique position to help millions of other people to do the same.

Everything's getting better, most of the time, in most places — and that's what's really causing most of the anxiety.

By any material standard, life for most people is much better than it was even 25 years ago. We live in an "age of affluence" marked by unprecedented living conditions.[3] The global collapse of communism and other socialist-based experiments has released creative and productive forces in most regions. Fewer wars are taking place, with fewer casualties than at any time in the last 500 years. Medical technology, organization, and treatments are becoming available to most people in most places. The number of countries ruled by elected democracies is increasing, while those ruled autocratically are declining.

Wealth is up, poverty is down. Except for those in some areas of the Middle East and Africa, most people on the planet have seen their incomes increase significantly. Billions of people around the world are overcoming the old ravages of "scarcity" — especially in developing countries such as India and China. The application of microchip-based technologies to all economic sectors is creating wealth at unprecedented rates of growth.

Talking and traveling. Cheap, easy to-use cell phones have proliferated in every country, allowing hundreds of millions to bypass the need for central bureaucracies and land lines. The costs of airline, automobile, ship, and train travel have dropped dramatically, empowering people to become increasingly more mobile. The increasing accessibility to computers has opened up profound educational resources and access to information for people around the world.

Individuals freeing themselves. Even the most dormant and stagnant societies, with a few notable exceptions, are starting to stir. But it's on the individual level where the greatest energy and action are taking place. The introduction of microchip-based tools has equipped literally hundreds of millions of individuals around the world with the means for personal learning, growth, and progress.

Increasing numbers of men, women, and children are becoming Microchip-Friendly. Millions of individuals are moving toward The New Wealth and participating actively in The Transformation Agenda.

Even where ruling authorities are ruthlessly trying to prevent it, people in many places are freeing themselves of constraints on their imaginations, ambitions, opportunities, and capabilities.

Great progress is being made in most places as the dynamics of capitalism take hold, permitting greater rule of law and entrepreneurism.

And this is what is causing much of the anxiety. It's the good news that's actually the problem, not the bad news.

Competition, comparison, and anxiety. When you have an interconnected world where everybody knows what everybody else is doing, many types of anxiety result — especially related to economic progress and success. When people see that others are getting ahead economically, it can make them feel like they are falling behind. When they see other people enjoying more purposeful lives, it can make them feel that their lives lack meaning. When they begin to suspect that The New Wealth means much more than increased income and assets, they begin to fear that all of their money doesn't really matter. The following are some of the increasing anxieties people are expressing on their way from economic childhood to economic adulthood:

- **"We're losing touch with important things."** Everybody needs a set of ideals and values that provides them with meaning and purpose. The biggest problem is that many people do not have an energizing central belief system that they can relate their new experiences to. For much of human history, religious authority supplied this belief system and structured people's entire world view. Now, in our increasingly "secular" age, people have more political, economic, and religious freedom than ever before. But without the sturdy moral horizon that something like religious authority can provide, many people feel incomplete.

- **"Nothing seems stable."** Even the most educated and connected people can be overwhelmed by changes they don't understand. The amount of knowledge about new things in the world doubles every year or so. What seems familiar in people's lives keeps being disrupted and undermined by things that are unexpected and unpredictable. People find themselves pushed and pulled in all directions by this constant global change.

- **"It's hard to connect with what's going on."** People today have to spend an enormous amount of time outside of their "comfort zone," dealing with daily hassles that really aren't related to their goals and objectives. It's hard to focus on what's really important when·so much of our time and energy is caught up dealing with less important things. Instead of being directed by their best aspirations and purposes, people feel the need to attend to things that seem urgent but have very little value to them.

- **"I'm worried about the future."** The most important question anyone can ask themselves is, "What has to happen for me to feel happy and energized about the next 25 years of my life?" Yet many people have difficulty answering this question and taking ownership over their personal future. They are incapable of visualizing a future bigger than the past. More and more, it seems that the future is too big, too complicated, and too strange to think about. Feeling overwhelmed, they aim small and underperform.

- **"I need to stand out from the crowd."** We live in a society that celebrates uniqueness and even demands that people express their individuality. This trend is empowering. But it also means that people are under enormous pressure to be unique and distinctive. Everybody has talents and attributes that make them unique, but discovering this uniqueness can be difficult and emotionally draining. People often fear that they don't know themselves as well as they should.

- **"Other people have knowledge and skills that I lack."** The grass definitely looks greener on the other side of a thousand different fences. The most successful people in the world — and their numbers seem to be growing — appear to be operating at a much higher level of capability. Less successful people don't know where this knowledge and skill comes from, and they don't know how to acquire it for themselves.

- **"Too many people have unfair advantages."** Many people are convinced that the game is stacked against them. Others are getting unfair breaks, and enjoying unfair benefits. There's cheating going on, and nobody's blowing the whistle. It's discouraging to believe that, no matter how hard you try, or how well you play the game, the people with unfair advantages will always come out on top.

- **"So many people are being left behind."** Around the world, it appears that those who already have a lot are getting even more, and those who don't have anything are losing all hope of things getting better. The world looks like it's getting worse in so many different ways. The people on top act like they don't care, and those on the bottom are being driven to extremes.

- **"My children aren't progressing fast enough."** People know that their children are under significant pressure to succeed in school, while also facing enormous peer-pressure and vulnerabilities to readily available drugs and alcohol. Many parents have more financial resources to address any problems their children run into, but they are often painfully aware that money is no substitute for quality family time, of which they have less and less.

- **"The world feels so risky."** For much of human history, people faced "survival risks" from things like crop failures, droughts, epidemics, and fires. Billions of people have now overcome these risks, but that doesn't mean their lives feel any less risky. The social theorist Ulrich Beck uses the term "risk society" to describe our technologically advanced and highly global world.[4] Current risks include the transnational environmental risks associated with pollution, global warming, and pandemics like avian flu.

  In recent years, people have also faced great risks to their personal security from terrorism, nuclear proliferation, and the threat of biological or chemical weapons. Many people have become psychologically conditioned to approach daily activities like riding on the subway as high-risk endeavors.

- **"The best parts of my life have already happened."** People experience an enormous amount of anxiety from the fear that their best days are behind them — that the future is something to be dreaded. Many people feel that life was more exciting, enjoyable, and meaningful ten or 20 years ago. The memories are precious and poignant. Nothing as exciting appears to be happening right now. And looking ahead, nothing seems as promising.

- **"I'm worried about dying too soon, or living too long."** We live in an age of unprecedented life expectancies. But no statistic can stop people from worrying about dying unexpectedly, before their time, and causing problems for the people around them. They also see others living too long, and causing another set of problems.

  Financial advisors can certainly relate to this concern. Indeed, planning for retirement can be difficult when people have no idea whether their retirement will last ten years or 40 years. For that reason, noted management scholar Peter Drucker recently suggested that providing protection against the financial risks of living too long might become the next big focus of the financial services industry.[5]

- **"I want to leave an enduring legacy."** Each of us wants to be remembered and celebrated as someone who contributed to society and made a distinguishing mark on the world. Few things are more unsettling to people than the fear that they have done nothing in their life worthy of being remembered. People are hiring personal historians to write their biography, along with photographers, video specialists, and artists to provide a visual record of their life.

But people still feel anxious that their legacy will be misrepresented or tarnished by things out of their control. These anxieties are especially present among older people who fear that time to secure their legacy is running out.

The Crossover Concerns represent a great opportunity for financial advisors who are entrepreneurial.

The anxieties just discussed make up what I call "The Crossover Concerns." They are unique, I believe, to a world where things are getting better in visible ways — but not for everyone equally. Different people have different concerns, and for some, they are more pressing. People have different information and knowledge about these issues, and different capabilities and resources to deal with them. But everyone living today experiences these concerns, in one form or another, as a regular part of life. For the first time in history, the global population is becoming unified in its anxieties. The reason for this is that technology is unifying our overall experiences in thousands of different ways. The great commentator on technological evolution, Jacques Ellul, pointed out the crucial difference of our age from all previous ones:

It used to be that different kinds of disconnected technologies were found inside of separate societies; now all of these societies find themselves inside of a single, global technological system that evolves through the aspirations and efforts of everyone on the planet.[6]

When more than six billion people are all striving within a single global system like the one we now have, the anxieties that make up The Crossover Concerns are a natural by-product. This is the state of our world from now on. Throughout the 21st century, the technological integration of global society will continue unabated. Millions of new capabilities and resources, both big and small, will emerge to support the self-improvement of billions around the world. We are already amazed at some of the new capabilities that are available to us at the beginning of the century. It's impossible to predict what will be possible 90 years from now. This much we do know, however: The opportunities for individuals to move from economic childhood to economic adulthood will continually speed up — along with the level of anxieties that these opportunities create.

21st-century realities of life. The Crossover Concerns, then, represent a great opportunity for value creation for those financial advisors who are entrepreneurial in both their attitudes and approaches. As is the case in all other areas of human skill, some advisors will be much more successful at this than others. The advisors who will most successfully take advantage of The Crossover Concerns are those who quickly understand the following realities of life in the 21st-century marketplace, which I call "The Early Adaptor Attitudes."

The Early Adaptor Attitudes.
1. "Creative inequality" as a value system. The industrial economies and societies of the last two centuries put an enormous emphasis on equality as a central value. All the attempts at installing socialism around the world were based on this value. Our new century, based on microtechnology, will, in many ways, emphasize just the opposite. Since technological innovation always disrupts existing relationships and structures, it also introduces greater amounts of inequality. But this represents a creative inequality; that is, it's not based on having more of what already exists, but rather on creating entirely new kinds of opportunities, capabilities, and value.

Creative inequality is not based on having a bigger piece of the existing pie, but rather on making the existing pie much bigger, and on continually making many more pies, all of them bigger than what now exists.

Early adaptors running ahead. Certain individuals are far more Microchip-Friendly than the people around them. They are able to achieve The New Wealth more quickly and completely than the general population. They are much more aware of The Transformation Agenda than others. As a result, these early adaptors will move ahead much more quickly — and this will be visible to everyone around them. They will not be bothered by the fact that things are unequal. They will thrive on the growing creative inequality within all sectors of global society. For them, equality is not the central value. For them, the central value in their lives is creativity — and the value creation that comes from it.

2. Individual life as an integrated and evolving whole. The Industrial Age put enormous emphasis on group solidarity, as was seen in trade union movements around the world. By the end of the 20th century, this emphasis on solidarity had taken the form of various kinds of gender, racial, ethnic, and cultural identifications. The age of the microchip goes in a completely different direction. The emphasis is now on the never-ending self-improvement of individuals, irrespective of their group affiliations.

We live in a world where individuals from a very early age can link up via the Internet with like-minded friends and collaborators around the world. Being successful and satisfied within this integrated world requires being an integrated individual who is always growing in knowledge and capability. The solidarity movements of the past two centuries were essentially collectives of economic children who were fearful about their limited securities in a world of scarcity.

In contrast, the movement toward economic adulthood made possible by microtechnology requires individuals to leave behind their group identifications and focus on the constant growth of their own personal capabilities.

The search for self-discovery and self-development that millions of people are undertaking is the most important social trend in the world today, and it has real marketplace implications for financial advisors — implications that we will discuss throughout this book.

3. Surrounded by Unique Ability® advisors and experts. During the best decades of the industrial era, millions of men and women had a sense that they were taken care of by the executives and managers of large bureaucratic organizations. Just securing employment in one of these organizations was to secure a lifetime of protections, guarantees, and comforts. Very little was missing. Very little else was called for. Then the microchip was introduced to economic life, and the process of global creative destruction quickly took hold. Within a quarter-century, most industrial protections and guarantees went out the door, and the comforts of the industrial life disappeared. The wise and caring management was nowhere to be found. It quickly became apparent that individuals were on their own, and that they needed outside help to create a secure and successful life. They needed skilled advisors and experts to help them plan and organize all of the crucial areas related to their careers and personal lives.

There is a direct correlation, then, within all societies between the decline of industrial bureaucracies and the increased need for independent advisors with specific Unique Abilities.

The farther individuals proceed through the crossover to economic adulthood, the more they need and make use of advisors and experts who can help them achieve all aspects of The New Wealth.

4. Growth is based on compound multipliers. Industrialization used machine power to dramatically increase the productivity of human labor. This breakthrough, further multiplied by the compounding power of expanding banking systems and stock markets, made it possible for great wealth to be created within advanced economies. The microchip revolution has increased these productivity and wealth multipliers to levels not dreamed of by the greatest industrialists and capitalists of the last century. The greatest practical knowledge on the planet today is an understanding of how to multiply human capabilities and resources through the use of microtechnology. Those who build their work, their lives, and their futures around this multiplier knowledge will continually advance more quickly than those who don't.

5. Multiplier advantages can be used to help others. The Industrial Age gave birth to philanthropy as a crucial way of improving living conditions within modern societies. But the organizational capabilities and financial resources of non-profit organizations in the last century will pale by comparison with those of the microchip age. In the decades ahead, tens of millions of individuals, with increasing surpluses of both time and money — and using entrepreneurial strategies — will bring about fundamental improvements in every sector of life.

It will become a normal attitude in the coming age of global abundance for successful and capable people to continually improve the world around them throughout their lives.

They will do this in millions of unpredictable ways, largely as a form of creative self-expression. Very little of this will be under the direction or control of the old bureaucratic organizations of the industrial era, which will decline and disintegrate.

6. Capitalism is expanded cooperation. Throughout the 21st century, those who think capitalism is a force for good in the world will enjoy much greater success and satisfaction than those who don't. This will leave behind significant numbers of individuals, many of them highly educated, who continue to believe that capitalism is a force of exploitation and oppression. These anti-capitalists are mistaken in their viewpoint, mainly because they don't understand the underlying dynamic that makes it such a powerful force of material progress.

Cooperation among strangers. F. A. Hayek, in his book, *The Fatal Conceit*, explains that the early opponents of capitalism, including Karl Marx, never recognized that the capitalist system grows through a process of expanded cooperation among strangers. The greater the cooperation, and the greater number of strangers who are involved, the more the system grows. *The striving for increased capital, then, is not the root cause of the capitalist system, but is a by-product of increased cooperation.*[7] Through the Internet, the microchip revolution makes increased cooperation among strangers the most powerful force for economic and political change in the world. This cooperation will grow exponentially, as will the amount of surplus capital that it creates as a by-product.

7. Everything successful will be done inside of a process. The Industrial Age was a world of products, more products than earlier times could ever have imagined. In the microchip age, there will be even more products, but the true nature of microtechnology actually lies in processes. Everywhere in the microchip world, new processes are being used to produce breakthroughs in the areas of science, other technology, communications, economics, politics, and cultural pursuits. All breakthroughs in the entire world of business will now be more in the area of processes than products. The world of the Internet, the greatest achievement of the microchip age so far, is an infinite web of processes — constantly integrating and continually expanding. For those individuals who understand how processes are created, changed, and improved, life in the 21st century is increasingly simple, stimulating, and enjoyable. For those who don't, it is mind-boggling and scary.

The most successful individuals and organizations of the 21st century, then, will be those who understand how to create and use Unique Processes for the purpose of ever-increased value creation in the world around them.

Becoming an economic adult requires a growing awareness of how to create processes for oneself and others. This self-improvement begins by making use of the Unique Processes that other people have already created.

8. This crossover period is historically unique. A period like the one we are living through, which I refer to as a Great Crossover, has occurred only three times before in human development. None of the previous crossovers — which corresponded to the evolution of speech, writing, and printing as new capabilities — involved the whole human population at the same time. And the size of our current population is exponentially greater than those that experienced the earlier crossovers. In the future, this period of the late 20th and early 21st centuries will be remembered as a crucial watershed in the evolution of human society. So there is a great deal of meaning, significance, and purpose to what we are living through.

Motivated to do great things. This is a great, historic time to be alive. People in the future will envy us for the experience that is available to us on a daily basis. The more we recognize and appreciate this, the more we will be motivated to do great things with the opportunities and resources this period affords us.

Understanding The Early Adaptor Attitudes puts advisors in a unique position to deal with The Crossover Concerns.

You can immediately see that The Early Adaptor Attitudes resonate with and reinforce the three conceptual tools from the previous section: Microchip-Friendly, The New Wealth, and The Transformative Agenda. But even more important, The Early Adaptor Attitudes put the financial advisors who make them the basis of their daily thinking into a unique position to help their clientele overcome the anxieties of The Great Crossover. By becoming comfortable, right now, with the central values and requirements of the microchip age, advisors can successfully lay out a plan and path that continually takes their clients and customers toward economic adulthood. As I will explain in a later section, these plans and paths will all be developed inside of Unique Processes that continually adjust to each client's unique issues and progress. *These Unique Processes will provide clients with freedom from the anxieties of our age — and for providing this freedom, advisors will be extraordinarily well paid.*

Long suffering, short suffering. In The Strategic Coach Program, I always tell my entrepreneurial participants that every change requires suffering of some kind. The only question remains, is it going to be long suffering, or short? Right now, the entire global population is experiencing the suffering that comes with making The Great Crossover to economic adulthood. The Crossover Concerns, those anxieties that everyone on the planet is experiencing to one degree or another, are not pleasant to endure, especially when there seems to be no end in sight. The great opportunity for financial advisors is to show that anxiety can be relieved quite quickly — and then to provide the means for their clientele to achieve the increased clarity, confidence, and capability that will make it so. Economic adulthood requires suffering, but the suffering can be short. Financial advisors who are true entrepreneurs — who have made The Early Adaptor Attitudes their own, are primed to make this possible. No other professionals in the 21st century are in a position to do this so directly or so well.

Opportunity 3:
Simplifying Complexity

Few individuals today have been educated and trained to deal with the complexities of living in the microchip-based world of the 21st century. Fewer still have the natural attitudes and abilities to live easily and happily with the unpredictability caused by never-ending technological change. Of course, those who are thriving on this complexity are winning in extraordinary ways. This is a period of tremendous opportunities and rewards for them. They love the world they are living in, and can't imagine a better time to be alive.

But for those who can't cope, or who find it manageable but fatiguing, it's an overwhelming and mostly negative experience. What has occurred technologically over the past three decades is not just different in degree from previous times. It's different in kind — a radical departure from the way individual and collective life used to be experienced. Various institutions and structures that shielded people from the impact of change — governments, religions, corporations, unions, cultural organizations, and social associations, for example — no longer provide protection. Or, if they do, they do so in ways that leave people unsatisfied and uncertain about their personal futures.

It's increasingly apparent that millions — soon to be billions — of men, women, and children are looking for innovative solutions to help them live successfully in a radically different kind of world.

The problems of complexity are the biggest opportunities of the 21st-century economy and society.

Complexity is the central issue of our time. No one on the planet is immune to its impact and implications. People's success and satisfaction in life, the advantages they enjoy, and their status in society are all determined by their ability to deal with complexity. Everybody has decisions to make, relationships to manage, and "messes" to clean up. Everybody has extraordinary demands on their time and energy. And therein lies a great opportunity for entrepreneurial financial advisors to be extraordinarily useful to millions of potential clients.

What clients want more than anything from you is sanctuary — relief from the constant complexities that are overwhelming them.

Here are four common sources of complexity that frustrate people seeking financial advice.

- **Complexities of information:** Organizations used to have rooms entirely devoted to storing information. Now, all of that information can be stored on a microchip. People have an unprecedented ability to generate constant streams of new information and package it in new content forms. In our 24/7 electronic age, "information overload" has become a reality for many people. Processing all the information takes up an enormous amount of energy. People can find it difficult to weed through all the distractions and focus on the things that are truly meaningful in their lives.

- **Complexities of choice:** One of the by-products of an information society is that it magnifies the choices available to people. Everywhere, choice is abundant. But when people have too many options, they can easily feel overwhelmed. Choice forces people to make difficult trade-offs between competing preferences. People often feel pressured to make the "right" choice, yet they can't seem to grasp the larger "purpose" behind their choices.

- **Complexities of time:** For today's "economic adults," time is the scarcest resource of all. People face unprecedented demands on their time from a variety of sources. They work longer hours, while having to manage family life. More important, they are being forced to spend time overseeing tasks such as financial planning that used to be taken care of by large organizations.

- **Complexities of finances:** We live in an age where trillions of dollars flow electronically around the world in a matter of seconds. People with mutual funds and actively traded portfolios can find their assets change hands on a daily basis. In these circumstances, people have enormous difficulty developing a sense of attachment to their assets, many of which are tied up in companies that people have no sense of relationship with, and whose operations they hardly understand.

Without this sense of familiarity, the financial realm becomes incredibly complex and abstract to people. Many people simply don't enjoy dealing with finances, nor do they have the knowledge and comfort-level that financial advisors bring to these issues. Because they are being asked to make more financial decisions, they feel incredibly anxious about making the wrong decisions and jeopardizing their financial future.

Developing "Complexity Consciousness."
In order for advisors to take advantage of complexity, they have to first develop what I call Complexity Consciousness. This represents a very different way of looking at the world and at daily life. When an advisor adopts this perspective, significant new opportunities and capabilities immediately become possible. There are ten parts to this new perspective:

1. The world is now an infinite complexity-creating system.
Everyone is increasingly involved in technological activities, but no one is in charge. Everyone sees some benefit for themselves in new technological tools and systems, but almost no one comprehends what the next breakthroughs will be. The microchip makes it possible for technologies in all fields of activity to be linked together. This makes everything more complex. These connected technologies expand across national borders, and all countries become connected by technology, and dependent upon its usefulness. This also increases complexity in the world. Each new microchip breakthrough gives rise to new

systems, which are then integrated with existing systems. One area of complexity now multiplies all other areas. These new tools and systems are applied to every area of human activity — in all sectors of science, economics, politics, culture, and social development — and each application gives rise to still newer possibilities. The bottom line: *The overall complexity in the world is now feeding on itself to create even greater complexity.*

I could go on with this description of how microtechnology propagates itself throughout the world, but most people living in modern societies are familiar with the experience. From now on, we all live in a world that is an unstoppable complexity-creating system.

You might ask at this point, "What does this have to do with being a financial advisor in the 21st century?" Just this: Financial advisors, because of their combination of skills in finances and human psychology, and their ability to form long-term, personal relationships with their clientele, are ideally positioned to help people deal with the dangers and opportunities caused by increased complexity. In fact, there is no other profession that can be more useful. But for this usefulness to be realized, financial advisors must understand what is happening with the individuals they are dealing with. The first thing they have to understand is the importance of "The Ceiling of Complexity."

2. Every individual has a built-in Ceiling of Complexity that determines personal learning, growth, and success. There is a breathtaking amount of inequality in the world. You can see it between cultures, between countries, between cities, between corporations, and between groups of people — and you can see it between individuals. The cause of all this inequality lies in the unequal ability to deal with complexity. This, more than any other single factor, is the reason why some people are successful in today's world, while others are failing. Successful people, societies, and cultures are first and foremost successful at dealing with the complexity in their lives. Those who are struggling are doing a poor job of dealing with the complexity in theirs.

In the same family, with individuals raised under more or less the same conditions, you can have some members who are successful with complexity and others who are failing. A sister looks at the world of technological change and sees nothing but opportunities, while her younger brother sees nothing but dangers. She is motivated to grow, while he is fearful and paralyzed. What separates these siblings is their differing abilities to deal with complexity.

The Ceiling of Complexity™. Complexity is something that each individual faces alone. It is an individual issue because every person has a completely different Ceiling of Complexity. This ceiling determines how much complexity you can handle on a continual basis over the course of your life. It also determines how quickly you can adjust to new circumstances and recognize new possibilities, and how well you can master new situations.

The winners. In some individuals, The Ceiling of Complexity is extraordinarily high. These are the people who thrive in today's world. They love innovation, change, and unpredictability. They find the increased complexity caused by microtechnology both stimulating and challenging. They can't imagine a better world to be in. Their ability to handle complexity keeps them on top of things. They are the first to see new opportunities and the first to take advantage of them. In every situation, they are likely to be the winners. Because they are successful, they are confident about their abilities and look forward to the future with optimism. They are confident that things are always going to get better because they have the ability to keep getting better themselves.

Not only do these winners have a high Ceiling of Complexity, they also have the ability to keep raising it.

The losers. Of course, we know many people who are just the opposite. They have a very low Ceiling of Complexity. Virtually any kind of change in the world around them is a threat. Their ability to change is minimal. Their overall attitude toward life is that of a victim. They find much of what is going on in the world around them oppressive. They are defensive and reactive on a regular basis. They blame others for their predicament and are often filled with anger, envy, and resentment toward those who are winning. They view these people as oppressors. Between these two extremes is everyone else on the planet. Every person has a Ceiling of Complexity that determines his or her ability to learn, grow, and succeed. Each of us is on our own individual track with regard to this ability. For some of us, our life's activity always involves raising our Ceiling of Complexity to a higher level. For others, the ceiling becomes fixed at a certain level and never goes any higher.

The principal role of financial advisors in this century, then, will be to create the financial and psychological opportunities that motivate large numbers of individuals to keep raising their Ceiling of Complexity throughout their lives. This will enable people to make The Great Crossover. It's important to have a critical mass of the population moving forward like this because many individuals will either be incapable of doing so — or will refuse to do so.

3. Complexity creates increased confusion, isolation, and powerlessness in those who can't deal with it. Many observers of modern life have described the contradiction of individuals feeling utterly alone despite being surrounded by many other people. This condition is caused by having a low Ceiling of Complexity. The daily news is filled with reports of people suffering mental and emotional breakdowns, also the result of having a low ceiling. Within prosperous countries, there is a growing number of "dropouts," individuals who have stopped trying, who don't seem to care about anyone or anything. Around the world, there is conflict, bloodshed, and destruction in numerous places. Again, the root cause of these situations is a low Ceiling of Complexity. For large numbers of people in every part of the world, the expanding technological system is causing more change than they can handle. There is far too much complexity for them to think straight. They think the wrong thoughts, make bad decisions, communicate in counterproductive ways, and continually act out in ways that set them farther back.

Just enough to cope. Even among people who seem to be doing okay, many of these problems and dangers are just around the corner. Their Ceiling of Complexity is just barely high enough to let them cope. They have some sense of direction, but a great deal of life is confusing. They have some confidence, but more often than not, they feel isolated. They have some capabilities, but in the face of many challenges, they feel powerless.

Around the world, then, we are all involved in this central reality of being alone with our individual Ceiling of Complexity.

With natural aptitude, luck, and conscious improvement, many of us are able to raise our ceiling throughout our lives. The world keeps getting more complex, and our ability to deal with complexity keeps growing. But for many people, this is never going to happen. There are casualties of complexity all around us, and there will be many more in the future. Some individuals, because of their intellectual and emotional make-up, will never be able to raise their ceiling. Others, because of their negative beliefs about the technological world, and about their lives within it, will adamantly refuse to do so.

Eager but ignorant. The vast majority of individuals, however, if they knew how, would be eager to learn how to raise their Ceiling of Complexity. They would be willing to do this continually over the course of their lives. What they are lacking are new strategies and tools for doing so. They need new kinds of teachers and guides to show the way. They need new structures and processes to support their improvement, progress, and growth.

Financial advisors, to take advantage of the opportunities brought about by increased complexity, need to lead the way as role models who demonstrate the ability to keep raising their Ceiling of Complexity over the course of an entire lifetime. Advisors with this ability will be able to help their clientele escape from the dependencies of the old industrial society. They will enable their clients to free themselves from the anxieties associated with The Great Crossover from the Industrial Age to the age of microtechnology.

4. All dependencies and anxieties come from an inability to deal with growing complexity in one's world. When people feel dependent, it's for a very good reason. They need someone or something else to protect them from the challenges of growing complexity in the world. A frequent conversation I have with my entrepreneurial clients relates to why some people spend their whole lives doing boring, frustrating, and unsatisfying work inside large bureaucratic corporations and institutions. They ask, "Why would anyone do that?" The answer is simple: The bureaucracies protect these people from having to deal directly with complexity in the outside world. Millions, perhaps billions, of people around the world today lack the ability to deal with complexity in an entrepreneurial fashion. Their Ceiling of Complexity is not high enough. They lack the ability to take their ceilings higher. They need protections and guarantees to make their lives feel safer. These protections are not only physical and financial, but emotional and psychological.

Not alone. It's not just bureaucracies that provide these, but belief systems and communities of many different kinds. People need to feel that they're not alone with complexity. They need to feel that they are being taken care of, that other people are looking out for them, that other people care. They want to have a sense of direction, and they can't provide this for themselves. They want to feel confident, but they don't know how to do this on their own. They want to feel capable, but they need others to provide them with capabilities. They simply can't deal with all the complexity of the world straight on.

The anxieties of our age arise largely because people don't feel protected and safe in the face of increased complexity.

Cutting off and opting out. Complexity, as an experience, is marked by surprise and speed, and also by disturbance and disruption. All of these produce anxiety. New things are happening that we don't understand. We can't keep up with all these new things. What we thought was normal is called into question, and what we found comfortable and reassuring no longer is. All of these things make us anxious, and they are all the result of increased complexity caused by the evolution of microtechnology.

Many people find it so difficult to deal with greater complexity in the world that they try to cut themselves off from it by various means. They attempt to create or move to places where the pace is slower. They stop listening to the news and stop talking to people who bring up new subjects. They use drugs of one kind or another to keep themselves feeling tranquil, connected to others, artificially confident, or oblivious to the complexities of the world around them. They join big causes or movements that offer a single, big answer that relieves them from the need for personal improvement and change. They take refuge in various kinds of nostalgia or fantasy. Or they use different kinds of trivial pursuits — including forms of consumption, recreation, and entertainment — to take up all their time and attention. *These strategies are understandable if we see them as attempts to deaden the anxieties of living in a complex world that seems out of control.*

Dealing with the world straight on. For all of those who are trying to avoid dealing with complexity, there are just as many who want to raise their Ceiling of Complexity. They want to get better at dealing with this technological world. They're trying to increase their sense of direction, confidence, and capability in response to changing conditions. They want to deal with the 21st-century world straight on and are looking for experts who will help them to do this.

Not all financial advisors are capable of playing this role. Many are deeply dependent upon bureaucracy and are as anxiety-filled as the people they're trying to help. But there is also an emerging group of advisors around the world who are entrepreneurial in both their careers and in their personal lives. Their greatest motivation is increased freedom, and this has led to continual learning and growth. They have raised their own Ceiling of Complexity and have learned how to do this on a continual basis. They have also come to understand that complexity itself is the raw material for creating new kinds of value for their clientele.

"Transformation of complexity" is the sector of the global economy where the greatest opportunities for financial advisors are emerging.

The first four parts of the Complexity Consciousness described the general conditions of complexity in today's world. These conditions affect everyone in a variety of ways. Dealing with all the different by-products of complexity is now a major focus of everyday life for most people. Having established this context, we can now focus more specifically on the opportunities that complexity offers to entrepreneurial financial advisors during the decades ahead. We'll start by thinking about complexity in a new way.

5. Complexity is the raw material for creating opportunity and value in all areas of human experience. The idea of complexity as a raw material is a new idea. This wouldn't have been talked about 50 years ago, or even 30. Most people see complexity as a problem, something to be avoided and eliminated. They don't see it as something highly valuable and desirable. Let me explain why I do.

My own analysis from coaching entrepreneurs over the past three decades is that complexity is not only something to be viewed positively, but is the single most important resource for creating new value in all market-places in the 21st century.

I have some evidence to back up this contention, in the form of four significant changes taking place in modern societies.

- **Turmoil in the microchip-specific industries:** Since the microchip was invented in the 1960s, all the industries directly related to utilizing this innovation have been in a constant state of turmoil. Each new breakthrough enables many others to raise their Ceiling of Complexity. The microchip-specific industries both produce greater complexity and feed on it. The creative destruction turmoil in this one sector of the global economy continually causes shock waves of turmoil in other sectors.

- **Expansion of the service sector:** As new generations of microchip-based technologies enter the marketplace, society requires a greater range of services to deal with the increased complexity. The service sectors in the U.S., Canada, and the U.K. have expanded from less than 40 percent of GDP in 1950 to more than 70 percent in 2007. All other developed countries are showing the same trend. Even old-line commodities and manufacturing sectors are surviving and succeeding by utilizing microchip-based innovations and new types of services.

- **Growth of the "experience" sector:** Microtechnology makes everything it touches more complex, including every aspect of work and lifestyle. This impact increases the anxiety levels of the millions of people who are directly affected and their families. In order to find relief from increasing complexity, these individuals turn to a growing number of "experiences" that promise to be intellectually stimulating, psychologically rejuvenating, and emotionally satisfying. These can take the form of custom-designed and uniquely packaged vacations, shopping junkets, leisure therapies, hospitality adventures, or educational programs catering to myriad interests. The "experience" sector is the fastest growing segment of advanced economies.[8] People need special experiences of every kind in order to protect themselves against the complexity caused by technology.

- **Emergence of the "transformation" sector:** A "transformation" is any experience in which an individual feels that his or her Ceiling of Complexity has been raised. The most valuable kind of experience a person can have in today's world is a transformation that increases their ability to raise their ceiling in the future. *Self-improvement and growth is so crucial to millions of individuals in the 21st century that they will pay a premium to experience it.*

Can't make the crossover without it. Of all the capabilities that people can acquire in a complexity-creating world, this capability for transformation is the most important one. People can't go from economic childhood to economic adulthood without it. They will adjust all aspects of their working and personal lives to utilize and increase this capability. "Transformation" is the sector of the global economy where the greatest opportunities are emerging, and where the highest prices can be charged. Very few people at present have identified this reality and the opportunities that go with it.

Making the crossover from childhood to adulthood is a transformative experience that lasts a lifetime. On their own, few people know how to create this experience. This, clearly, is where financial advisors come to the fore.

6. Using complexity as a strategy, and simplicity as a tool. Complexity is now a universal experience. By that I mean that it affects everyone and becomes the one issue that unifies our experience of daily life in the 21st century. Everyone, simply by being in this world, now deals with greater amounts of complexity from one year to the next. The amount of complexity that we face will always be greater. It will never be less. Because microtechnology keeps connecting more people, the complexity of our lives, and our world, keeps growing exponentially.

Each individual has a personal Ceiling of Complexity that makes daily life enjoyable or miserable, exciting or scary, promising or discouraging.

The most important problems of the century are all complexity problems. The most important solutions are solutions to complexity. The most successful people are those who can transform complexity into simplicity on a continual basis. The least successful are those who can't. The most progressive and dynamic organizations are those that utilize complexity as a resource and opportunity. The declining and disintegrating organizations are those that can't. The most successful countries and societies are those that thrive on complexity. The failures are those who can't.

Simplify yourself, then others. With this in mind, anyone who wants to be successful in both personal and professional life from this point forward needs to have complexity as his or her central focus. The strategy is, first, to look for complexity in one's own life and simplify it. With the direction, confidence, and capability that come from doing this, the next strategy is to look for complexity in other people's lives and transform it into simplicity. This ability to continually transform complexity into simplicity will be our most important skill over the next hundred years.

7. The most useful and profitable role for financial advisors lies in being lifetime simplifiers for their clientele. Most people think that financial services is about money, but actually it's about complexity. Most financial advisors think their most important job is to help their clientele with money, but actually it's to help their clientele with the different kinds of complexities of living in a world governed by the evolution of microtechnology. *As a financial advisor, therefore, if you start with complexity as the focus of your strategy, the money part of the business becomes increasingly simple.*

Radically different futures. If, on the other hand, you start with money as your focus, the complexity of the world — and the financial services industry — will always be overwhelming. From our experience in dealing with both entrepreneurial advisors and those who are "captive" to large bureaucratic organizations, we can see two radically different futures. The "captive" advisors, who are forced by their bureaucratic dependency to focus increasingly on the money, are beset by ever increasing problems of complexity. Their future always looks more complicated, filled with conflicts and confusion. The entrepreneurial advisors, who focus on addressing complexity as their main strategy, look at the future becoming simpler and more enjoyable. They see their role as lifetime simplifiers for their clientele. It's a role that always becomes more valuable and rewarding.

8. Achieving a simple sense of direction, confidence, and capability where others are overwhelmed by complexity. Throughout this book, we argue that financial advisors must excel at simplifying their own lives so they can then do the same for their clientele. An advisor who is limited by a low personal Ceiling of Complexity cannot be of much help in the marketplace.

The most he or she can do is peddle commoditized products designed by others. These products don't do much to reduce complexity in the lives of clients. In most cases, because they are unsatisfactory solutions, they add to it.

Advisors who are restricted in this commoditized way lead lives that are increasingly complex and conflicted from one year to the next. Each year, they are forced to deal with more technological, bureaucratic, and legal issues that have nothing to do with creating value or earning income. Each year, their productivity declines and their frustration increases.

Clients and customers increasingly sense this limitation in commodity-based advisors and don't place much value on what such individuals can do for them. They're looking for advisors who have their own act together when it comes to transforming complexity. They want advisors who have a sense of clear personal direction amidst the confusion of technological society. They want advisors who feel personally confident about the future, and who seem to have ever increasing capabilities for eliminating the anxieties of this crossover period.

We're talking here, of course, about financial advisors who are entrepreneurs, who are not trapped within bureaucratic structures. We're talking about individuals who have the freedom to put their clients first, without having to think about the priorities of some bureaucratic organization. We're talking about financial advisors who understand that their greatest value is in continually making their clientele's lives simple in a world of ever increasing complexity. And, finally, we're talking about financial advisors who have developed a unique value creation offering in the marketplace that is based on personal wisdom and a unique problem-solving process — not on the sale of off-the-shelf commoditized products and services.

9. Creating knowledge and wisdom in a world that is overwhelmed by data and information. Individuals who have a low Ceiling of Complexity often feel that they do not have enough data and information. Paralyzed by the complexity of the decisions they have to make, they invariably try to rectify this by taking on even greater complexity by seeking out even more data and information. In other words, they're trying to fight fires with gasoline. The biggest problem for most people in modern societies is that they have too much information and very little knowledge and wisdom. They have an overabundance of disconnected facts and no way to see everything as a whole. Immersed in a flood of details, they have no way of seeing a simple path forward. They lack both the knowledge necessary to understand their situation and the wisdom to see how they can improve it.

This is where a great opportunity lies for entrepreneurial financial advisors: their continual creation of strategic knowledge and wisdom that raises each client's unique Ceiling of Complexity.

Clients and customers will always pay a premium for this kind of service and solution. They will always value this kind of knowledge and wisdom the most. They will also value above everyone else the advisors who can provide this for them. They don't need more data and information. They already have too much, and it is confusing them. What they want are unique ways of thinking about their own complexity — and a custom-designed plan that continually moves them to greater simplicity in all areas of their lives.

10. Developing a lifetime simplifying capability. This last point regarding complexity provides a bridge to Part 2 of the book, which focuses on Freedom. In this initial Opportunity section, we have suggested that the three greatest breakthroughs for financial advisors in the 21st century relate to dependency, anxiety, and complexity. These are the overriding sources of danger that virtually all individuals now experience in a world governed by the evolution of the microchip. To the degree that the clientele of financial advisors deal with these dangers successfully, they will have successful futures. To the degree that they fail, their lives will be less successful in many different ways.

The lifetime capability to simplify. In the years ahead, as the microchip goes about its incessant work of bringing greater complexity into everyone's lives, an entirely new kind of capability is required to be a successful financial advisor. This capability is called a Unique Process.

A Unique Process is uniquely organized and packaged wisdom — based on successful experience and financial expertise — that enables any client going through the process to examine and simplify every aspect of personal and business life.

This process is geared directly to the unique issues of each client, and continually evolves to support that individual's growing successes and aspirations over an entire lifetime. Only those financial advisors who develop a Unique Process as the basis of their work in the marketplace will be able to solve their own complexity issues in the years ahead. By successfully solving their own situation, they will then have unlimited opportunity to help the very best clientele in the years ahead to solve theirs.

2.

A Century Of Freedom For Entrepreneurial Advisors

The
Advisor
Century

Part 2:
A Century Of Freedom
For Entrepreneurial Advisors

I've been coaching entrepreneurs since 1974, more than 11,000 individuals from 60 different industries around the world. Although these men and women differ from one another in many ways, they have one thing in common: Their greatest motivation is the desire for more freedom. This is especially true of those entrepreneurs who are financial advisors. During the early years of my coaching career, I worked with clients in many different situations, including corporate and government, as well as non-profit executives and managers. I quickly decided to focus just on those who were entrepreneurial in their attitudes, activities, and aspirations. My reason was that I discovered that entrepreneurs are unique in their potential to realize four important freedoms.

- **Time:** *Entrepreneurs can continually increase their control of their professional and personal time.* Individuals who work in corporations or in government are not capable of doing this. At some point, of course, they can control their personal time, but only after they retire.

- **Money:** *There are no external limitations to how much income entrepreneurs can earn and how much wealth they can create — it's largely a matter of their ambitions and capabilities.* Individuals in other situations are restricted to salaries that are fixed by others. Even if they get bonuses, these, too, are determined by other people.

- **Relationship:** *Over time, entrepreneurs can design their work lives so they deal only with people who are agreeable to them.* In other settings, people are constrained to deal with those who come with the job or position. Part of what a lot of people are paid for in bureaucratic situations is putting up with other individuals who are unpleasant and uncooperative.

- **Purpose:** *Entrepreneurs can focus all their resources, capabilities, and opportunities on purposes of their own choosing.* In non-entrepreneurial situations, individuals must focus on other people's purposes in their work lives. Their own purposes are consigned to their personal lives.

These four freedoms are the raw material for the personal planning and improvement of the thousands of financial advisors in The Strategic Coach Program. Every quarter, they examine all aspects of their professional and personal lives and identify specific areas where they can become more free. The freedoms are not isolated from one another. Progress in one area immediately supports progress in the other three. The experience of making progress in all four areas is intoxicating and habit-forming. *Once an advisor has tasted freedom, he or she always wants more. Even as little as a year of making progress in this way is usually enough to make it a lifetime passion.*

For the rest of this section I am going to talk about the crucial factors that determine whether a financial advisor can continually increase his or her personal and professional freedom.

Freedom from, freedom to. When advisors first begin to seek greater freedom, the central focus is on liberating themselves from restrictions and limitations. There are immediate daily obstacles and constraints that annoy and frustrate them. The first decisions, plans, and actions that these advisors undertake are usually to overcome and remove these obstacles and constraints. But as this process of "freedom from" meets with real success, the focus turns to the second stage, "freedom to."

Over the years, I have worked with many financial advisors who are familiar with the Book of Exodus in the Bible. I tell them, "The skills that get you out of Egypt aren't the ones that get you into the Promised Land." There's one set

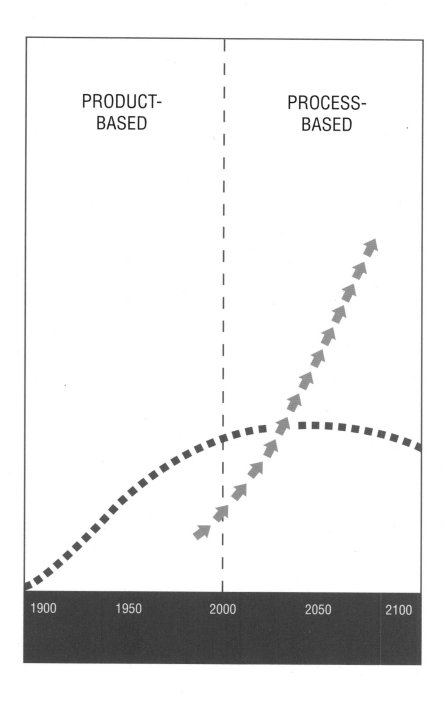

of attitudes and capabilities that is necessary for freeing yourself from undesirable and unsatisfying conditions. But a whole different set of attitudes and capabilities is required for you to truly enjoy a deeply valuable, significant, and satisfying life.

Boxed in for life. Most people in modern societies can still only fantasize about these freedoms. Compared with entrepreneurs, they have very little freedom of time, money, relationship, or purpose. Their lives are boxed in on many sides. These men and women earn a living by selling much of their waking time over many decades to employers who place limits on their earnings. They are constrained to deal with everyone their jobs require them to, agreeable or not, and they are expected to devote their energies largely to their employers' and other people's purposes, not their own. The conditions in which they work can be good or bad. They can be pleasant, stimulating, and rewarding — or boring, fatiguing, and exploitative. But either way, control over their situation is not theirs to demand or design. The average person who has spent their working life as an employee cannot imagine how work could be any other way. Without a taste of entrepreneurial freedom, it's hard to dream of a different life.

Being boxed in has been the situation for most people, forever. But microtechnology is changing things rapidly. For instance, as individuals access the Internet, they become aware of many different ways of making a living, nearly all of them entrepreneurial. As an interesting comparison between new times and old, the number of individuals who make their full-time living buying and selling on eBay is more than twice the number who work for General Motors. Ten years from now, GM will probably employ half the number of people it does today. On the other hand, Internet-based enterprises like eBay will have many millions more involved in entrepreneurial careers. The Great Crossover from economic childhood (working for GM) to economic adulthood (utilizing eBay) is being facilitated by the new capabilities, resources, and opportunities provided by microtechnology.

Besides these developments that are directly tied to the Internet, there are ten times as many entrepreneurial ventures being created by the application of microchip-based tools and systems to innovations and inventions throughout the economy. These trends are taking place everywhere, not just in developed countries, but in many underdeveloped places, which until recently were ruled by oppressive and backward political regimes. Everywhere, the desire for economic adulthood, based on an entrepreneurial approach to daily life, is prompting tens of millions of individuals to set out on the crossover. *The big motivation at the core of the crossover, I believe, is neither the money nor the technology, but the promise of dramatically greater freedom of time, money, relationship, and purpose.*

Potential, not actual, freedoms. Though all entrepreneurs have the unique potential to enjoy these four freedoms, they are not a given. Many entrepreneurs, and especially the hundreds of thousands who work in the financial services industry, are not actualizing their freedoms. Many financial advisors' control over their time, money, relationships, and purposes is actually decreasing. This is especially true for all those who have direct relationships with large financial bureaucracies. *I call these individuals "captive" advisors because they have signed contracts that continually take away their freedom as entrepreneurs.*

Increased restrictions, reduced capabilities. The reality is that thousands of "captive" advisors are facing an increasingly intrusive, demeaning, overbearing, and stifling compliance regime. They are increasingly seeing their every action regulated and monitored. They are increasingly prevented from doing anything creative or innovative. Many have been operating under restrictive and limiting conditions for so long that they can't see any possibility of greater freedom. For the most part, these captive advisors have traded opportunity for security, and growth for status — or, rather, they've made these trades for what they hope is security and status, because over time their situation within these large bureaucracies becomes tenuous. As their freedom to think, communicate, and act is restricted by bureaucratic superiors and lawyers, their competitive abilities in the marketplace are undermined. Throughout the English-speaking world, which employs the majority of experienced financial advisors, there has been a decade-long decimation of the ranks of those individuals who chose security and status over opportunity and growth. In the U.K., for example, since 1992, over 80 percent of captive advisors have been eliminated for reasons that will become clear throughout this book.

Over the same period, thousands of other advisors have had a dramatically different experience. The reason for this is that they have transformed their careers to be totally entrepreneurial within the context of a Unique Process. A Unique Process is a custom-designed thinking process based on a creative synthesis of your own wisdom and a client's most important aspirations. It is an expertly "packaged" sequence of actions that governs your relationship with clients at each stage of its development.

We will soon cover what it means to develop a Unique Process and operate as a Unique Process Advisor. But the important point here is that while captive advisors face an increasingly narrow future, Unique Process Advisors enjoy extraordinary opportunities that will enable them for the remainder of their careers to bypass all competitors and the restrictions of the industry itself. While every year captive advisors are living lives of greater complexity, Unique Process Advisors operate within a framework that makes both their business and their personal lives increasingly simple. While captive advisors are gradually losing their limited freedoms, Unique Process Advisors are continually enjoying greater freedom of time, money, relationship, and purpose.

The Unique Process as a permanent vehicle for advisor freedom in the 21st century.

For the remainder of this book, the discussion of expanded freedom for financial advisors will take place within the context of having a Unique Process that continually develops and expands as a powerful force in the marketplace. In order for this to be meaningful and useful to you, I will give several examples of advisors who have created powerful Unique Processes, and then describe what a Unique Process is and how it is created.

The Parent Care Solution[†††].

Transforming the relationships of adult children with their aging parents.
Dan Taylor, from Charlotte, North Carolina, was a lawyer before he became a financial advisor in the 1980s. Noticing that a great number of his baby boomer age clients were having difficulties dealing with the issues of their aging parents, he created a process called The Parent Care Solution. The process is based on six focused conversations that adult children and their parents can have about all the crucial questions, concerns, and decisions that relate to retirement, medical care, housing, daily support and assistance, financial controls, and legacies. By going through this process with the assistance of specially trained financial advisors, tens of millions of individuals in the decades ahead will avoid the misunderstandings, breakdowns in communication, estrangements, and tragedies that often undermine family relationships when adult children and their parents attempt to deal with these crucial issues. Not only has The Parent Care Solution enabled Dan Taylor to free himself from the restrictions and limitations of being a product-based advisor, but by licensing his Unique Process, he enables thousands of other advisors to gain greater freedom in their lives.

The Process for Protected Tomorrows*.

Transforming the lives of individuals with special needs and their families. More than one in ten families in the U.S. has a member — parent, spouse, sibling, or child — who is living with a condition requiring special care. The pressures that this places on family members, especially the parents of children with special needs, can be overwhelming. It can leave them exhausted and bankrupt. The structure of assistance to these families is largely bureaucratic, and therefore increasingly impersonal, ineffective, and deficient. Mary Anne Ehlert, a financial advisor with 30 years' experience, grew up in a family with a sister with severe disabilities and knows first-hand the difficulties that whole families endure. To provide a dramatic solution, Mary Anne created a Unique Process called The Process for Protected Tomorrows, which even in its early stages of development already provides the most comprehensive, high-quality system of support for both individuals with special needs and their families.

Stripping away all the bureaucratic and impersonal approaches, this Unique Process provides an economic foundation for solving each family's most pressing issues in a humane and caring fashion — and does so for the entire lifetime of the individual with special needs.

National impact. As was the case with Dan Taylor, Mary Anne Ehlert created her process first and foremost to free herself from the constraints of being a commodity-based advisor. Once she experienced the increased freedom and professional satisfaction that came from this decision, she saw the opportunity for helping other advisors make a similar move. The Process for Protected Tomorrows is now a formal structure that many other financial advisors across the U.S. license from Mary Anne's company. Based on success within her own industry, she is now expanding her training and licensing activities to the legal, medical, education, and social work sectors, as well as to retiring baby boomers.

The 90 Day Check-Up System[†].
Transforming individuals' lifetime confidence about their cash flow position.
As he was building his career as a financial advisor, Chuck Brewster noticed something about his successful clients. Although they were well-off from a net worth standpoint, very few of them had a handle on their cash flow situation. They were financially secure, but they didn't feel that way. The vast majority of them didn't have any measurement or reporting system that told them how they were making progress on a continual basis. This made them unskillful with their money. Because of their ignorance and anxiety in this area, they avoided making plans and decisions and taking strategic actions to improve their present situation and future prospects. After analyzing what was needed to rectify these deficiencies, Chuck created a computer-based Unique Process called The 90 Day Check-Up System. This process enables individuals to track 16 cash flow factors on a quarterly basis. Each session ends with a printed report and a plan of specific actions that will lead to improvement over the next 90 days.

From working with his clients, Chuck noticed immediately that when they became confident about their cash flow situation, they also became proactive about their overall financial situation. As soon as they understood how they were using their money, they began to take every aspect of their financial future more seriously. They established budgets and financial controls where these were lacking. They began to see the crucial importance of insurance. They began making better investments. Above all, they began establishing long-, medium-, and short-term plans for building the lives they wanted. Chuck also saw that his Unique Process could be easily utilized by other financial advisors. He created a user-friendly computer training program that has enabled hundreds of other advisors to master the basics of The 90 Day Check-Up System and begin using it successfully within two or three days. The advisors who are taking advantage of this new capability all report the same jump in confidence in their clientele that Chuck experienced with his.

Dan Taylor, Mary Anne Ehlert, and Chuck Brewster are just three examples out of hundreds of financial advisors who have developed their Unique Processes within The Strategic Coach Program. Thousands more will do so in the decades ahead. Although the three advisors we have spotlighted here began with a unique interest or concern in mind, the resulting Unique Processes that they have created reveal the following common characteristics and impacts.

Unique Processes are entirely client-focused. The three processes described above are all based on the needs of the clientele who utilize them — not on the advisor's financial needs or the financial goals of a corporate bureaucracy. All the information used to create the Unique Process comes from the client's issues, requirements, and aspirations. This means that advisors never lose touch with what their clients need and want.

No third party is involved or required in the Unique Process. Unlike the sale of regulated products, Unique Processes eliminate the need for a corporate third party to solve fundamental problems. All Unique Processes are based on in-depth conversations between advisors and their clientele. The problems are uncovered and their solutions are developed within these conversations. No outside party is required. This means that nothing that occurs outside of the advisor-client relationship can interfere with the effectiveness of the Unique Process.

Every Unique Process produces fundamental solutions. Every Unique Process focuses on solving the fundamental issues of dependency, anxiety, and complexity that clients are experiencing in their specific situations. Because individuals lead multi-dimensional lives, they may take advantage of many different kinds of Unique Processes to address all of their issues. These issues are at the core of life for everyone striving for success, satisfaction, and significance in the 21st century. They are at the core of moving toward economic adulthood. This means that advisors play increasingly important and valuable roles in the lives of their clients.

Unique Processes provide the framework for a complete organizational structure. Advisors with Unique Processes are able to build every aspect of their business and career around a single, evolving structure. The crucial impetus for change in a Unique Process is always new, more fundamental information about the clientele. All management and administrative activities inside the advisor's company are continually adjusted to reinforce the best solutions for clients' evolving issues.

Over time, the problem-solving capabilities of the Unique Process become more powerful. All hiring and training within the advisor's company is based on mastery of the different parts of the process. *This focus means that advisors can develop a highly successful business with a minimum of time spent on managing details and people.*

Unique Processes provide a single structure for advisors' career growth. Once the Unique Process is proven successful, the advisor can stay within its creative and productive structure for the remainder of his or her career. Regardless of what changes take place in society, in the economy, and within the financial services industry, the Unique Process always remains relevant, effective, and adaptable. *This feature alone eliminates enormous amounts of complexity for advisors in the 21st-century marketplace.*

Unique Processes relegate all products to the implementation stage. Unique Process Advisors utilize financial products to implement solutions that are designed within their conversations with clients. These implementations always occur at the end of the process, after a powerful trust relationship has been established between the advisor and client. *This means that Unique Process Advisors never sell products based on price — and never have to justify their product recommendations. It also means that the products they choose are only those that best bring about the transformative solutions needed by the client, as revealed in the Unique Process.*

Unique Processes are created and evolve outside of bureaucratic control. For those entrepreneurial advisors who are taking the Unique Process route, the biggest payoff is creative freedom. Every Unique Process is a creative amalgam of the clientele's fundamental concerns and issues and the advisor's life experience and wisdom as a problem solver. No other ingredients are required. The relationship between advisor and client falls under contract law, and bypasses bureaucratic and regulatory controls. *This means that once a Unique Process becomes successful in the marketplace, the advisor can — if he or she chooses — relinquish all product-based licenses and the complexity that accompanies them.*

Advisors are paid upfront for their Unique Process. One of the greatest sources of freedom in the Unique Process approach comes from advisors receiving advance payment. Every advisor brings a wealth of wisdom to his interaction with clients, but far too often, he treats this wisdom as an intangible value-added that can help him win a product sale. He gives everything away for free upfront and stakes everything on the outcome of the product sale.

In contrast, Unique Process Advisors are always paid upfront fees for the value they create. Clients commit to going through the process by writing a cheque. The size of these cheques increases as advisors gain greater problem-solving experience and reputation. When additional problem-solving tools are added to a Unique Process, additional payments are triggered.

In other words, advisors can continually set their fee to make a profit — raising the fee as their process evolves. Since their efficiency in implementing the Unique Process improves with each new client, profitability can keep growing.

These fees are in addition to any commissions earned from the sale of products used to implement the Unique Process. Indeed, we have found that advisors operating within a Unique Process continually experience far greater product sales than their commodity competitors. *This means that Unique Process Advisors have much greater cash flow certainty than product-based advisors — which leads to greater confidence of planning and investing in the growth of the advisors' companies.*

The Unique Process allows advisors to attract high-impact clients. All advisors know that time is money. The more time you have to spend on low-revenue activities, the less money you'll make. Yet many product-based advisors have to spend an inordinate amount of time on low-margin product sales. They have to invest a significant amount of time just to get business in the door, fill their account book, and maximize product transactions. They really have no systems in place to attract those "larger cheque" clients.

In contrast, Unique Process Advisors have a structure in place that continually allows them to attract and serve the highest-quality clients. They have the confidence and tools to approach these high-impact clients and win their business.

In other words, Unique Process Advisors are in a position to be selective about clients. We have continually found that people are willing to pay thousands of dollars in fees for the privilege of experiencing a powerful Unique Process. If clients balk at the fee, this reaction should be a red flag. If clients can't get over sticker shock, they probably aren't interested in what the advisor has to offer, and they probably aren't the kinds of clients that will help their business grow.

Unique Processes are proprietary intellectual property — and a Unique Process business has capital value. Unique Process Advisors own something substantial. Their processes are protected by intellectual property laws, which provide them with unique competitive advantages in the marketplace. This intellectual property can be licensed and sold, and the company based on this property continually increases in equity value. *Unlike the vast majority of product-based advisors who can only sell their cash flow streams and books of assets under management, Unique Process Advisors have real enterprises with unique assets.*

The Unique Process of one advisor can be combined with those of others to create powerful capability networks. The Unique Processes developed by entrepreneurial advisors within The Strategic Coach are based on common principles and structures. These features enable Unique Process Advisors to cooperate and create in an extraordinary fashion. There is a common Unique Process language that everyone understands. The building blocks used to construct one Unique Process are similar to those used to build all the others. *This means that dozens of Unique Process Advisors can build powerful entrepreneurial networks that provide comprehensive solutions for large numbers of clients — while allowing each advisor to retain professional independence.*

These characteristics are compelling reasons for an advisor to invest the time and effort to create a Unique Process. All of those who construct their future in this fashion will enjoy increased freedom of time, money, relationship, and purpose. They will be able to separate themselves from everything they find frustrating and constraining about just selling commoditized products. In other words, they will enjoy increased "freedom from."

At the same time, their Unique Process will add enormous purpose and motivation to their personal and professional lives. Their work will give them a sense of increased satisfaction and significance as they become more successful. Their efforts in the marketplace with their clientele will have a transformative impact on the lives of many individuals. The Unique Process, then, will also enable them to enjoy increased "freedom to."

The reason I advocate a Unique Process future for financial advisors is that there are a wide array of factors in the financial services industry that are threatening advisor freedom. *Without a Unique Process, it will become increasingly difficult for advisors to withstand the flood of bureaucratic and regulatory dictates coming their way.* They will find it more challenging to differentiate themselves in a marketplace where everyone is selling the same commoditized products and to build growing businesses in an environment where profit margins are unpredictable from one year to the next. And, above all, they will find themselves more and more hard-pressed to create value for clientele in a way that generates client loyalty and high-quality referrals.

Attributes of Unique Process Advisors.

As you read this description of the Unique Process as a vehicle for advisor freedom, you're probably saying to yourself, "This all sounds great, but what exactly is a Unique Process, and how do I create one?" In the next three sections, I am going to answer these two questions in considerable detail. Although it is much easier to create and continually improve a Unique Process within the framework of The Strategic Coach, I nevertheless know dozens of advisors who have developed highly effective processes on their own. Regardless of how you choose to do it, there are several things to keep in mind before you undertake a project that will last the remainder of your business career. You can only create a successful Unique Process if the following three things are true:

1. You value your own wisdom and experience more than anyone else's. All Unique Processes are a product of years of advisor learning and creativity. Advisors who take naturally to the idea of a Unique Process are those who have always been independent and innovative in their approach to their financial services work. From the very beginning, they saw better ways of serving their clients. They learned how to customize the commodities they were selling to the unique needs of their clientele. And they always learned far more from conversing with their clients than from any kind of formal education or training within the industry. They realized from an early point that head office administrators had little or no insight into the development of client relationships. They also realized that bureaucratic executives and industry regulators were largely ignorant when it came to the specific issues and concerns of their clientele, and that these individuals had priorities that didn't include them, their businesses, or their clientele. If all of these things describe you, then you will find it easier and more enjoyable to develop a Unique Process than will someone who is thinking about all of these things for the first time.

2. You value your clients and their lives more than your connections or agreements with any corporate or regulatory entities. Those who are Unique Process Advisors recognize that their clients' success is the key to all other success in their careers. They want to be instrumental in helping their clientele eliminate the dangers that are the source of their confusion and anxiety. They want to help these individuals capture all the opportunities that are available to them at any given time. And they want to reinforce the sense of confidence that their clients have about all aspects of their lives. More than anything, they want all of their clients to make The Great Crossover, the transition from economic childhood to economic adulthood. At the same time, they see their corporate and regulatory relationships within the financial services industry as utilitarian and temporary. They know from experience that the individuals who fill the jobs in corporate bureaucracies and regulatory agencies are there for short periods of time and are not to be depended upon for anything strategic or long-range. If these attitudes describe you, then the Unique Process path will be very beneficial.

3. You value your creative freedom more than your professional status and commodity-based security. All the advisors who have developed their Unique Processes in The Strategic Coach value personal and professional freedom more than any other condition or reward. Their prime motivation for entering the industry in the first place was to be more in control of their personal futures. Along the way, they realized that to be increasingly successful as professionals and increasingly useful to their clientele, they had to increase their operating freedom on a continual basis. As they developed their careers, they discovered that there were more obstacles than they had realized standing between them and the kinds of freedom that were necessary for their continued growth and improvement. *They learned that recognition and* *rewards are frequently offered to advisors within the bureaucratically-controlled industry in lieu of professional freedom.*

Much of their learning at a certain point focused on how to bypass these obstacles and inducements. When these advisors learned about the Unique Process, they jumped at the opportunity to satisfy all of their freedom requirements with a single strategy. As soon as they began using their Unique Process, they realized that this single structure, as it evolved, would continually provide them with increased freedom for as long as they were active in the marketplace. If these things are true about you, and if you are also deeply interested in satisfying your requirements for personal and professional freedom with a single strategy, then the Unique Process is right for you.

Now, let's move on to the three ways that the Unique Process can provide the increased freedom of time, money, relationship, and purpose that you are looking for.

Freedom 1:
Creating Intellectual Property

The single most important freedom that advisors require in the 21st century is the ability to create, own, and disseminate intellectual property. Any other freedoms they desire in their professional and personal lives depend on this first one. Among the thousands of financial advisors I talk with on an ongoing basis, this core issue of intellectual property is both the key to their excitement and satisfaction, and the key to their frustration and demoralization.

The degree to which they feel free as advisors is dependent on their developing and marketing intellectual property that they exclusively own. The degree to which they feel the opposite — captive and frustrated — is a result of their being prevented or prohibited from creating their own intellectual property.

Ownership of property equals freedom. The economist Hernando De Soto, in his book, *The Mystery of Capital,* points out that the only wealthy countries in the world are those that protect the private property of their citizens.[9] It's no coincidence that those same countries, in addition to freedom of property, also provide the greatest number of other freedoms. The freedom to own and develop private property, therefore, is the single most important factor in developing and maintaining free societies in which individuals can expand their capabilities to the fullest extent. The greatest creativity, cooperation, and productivity occur in those countries with the greatest protection of private property. For most of history, "property" has usually meant something material and tangible, but in the 21st century, the most valuable property is found in the realm of intellectual processes.

Power and control in the financial services industry lie in the ownership of Unique Processes.

The way the financial services industry developed over the past century-and-a-half was through organizations built around specific Unique Processes. Individual consumers increasingly looked for the assistance of financial companies and their sales forces to assist them in acquiring insurance and making investments. Along the way, the original processes that established the financial services industry remained more or less the same — until we reached the 1970s. At this point, the microchip became a fundamental tool for creating innovations within financial services companies. Over the past 30 years, the microchip revolution has brought about a number of changes that directly affected the activities and aspirations of financial advisors in the 21st century.

- **Free agency:** Microchip-based tools and systems available throughout the industry have enabled entrepreneurially-minded advisors to become independent operators in the marketplace. Advisors with computers, linked into a wide variety of data and information networks, can administer the details and manage the financial affairs of their clientele. In this way, advisors were freed from their dependency on the back office of the financial corporations.

- **Depersonalization:** Microchip technology has promoted an ever increasing depersonalization of the relationship between companies and their customers. The executives and managers within these companies ordinarily don't know any of the individual clients or customers — except for the most affluent. At the same time, the environments within large financial services companies have also become increasingly depersonalized. At all levels, from bottom to top, individuals are seen as replaceable, expendable parts. More emphasis is placed on job and career advancement than on value creation for the clientele. There has also been a "flattening" of most corporations, with fewer people doing more work. One outcome of this trend has been to off-load the servicing of customers, which used to be handled at head offices, to individual advisors.

- **Commoditization:** With the depersonalization of working relationships within financial services has come a commoditization of the "products" that the companies sell. It has become increasingly difficult for companies to differentiate their offerings in the marketplace. The window for profitability on products has grown shorter as the costs of marketing have increased. A winning formula for any particular Unique Process can be easily copied and duplicated by competitors. Since corporate loyalty has waned throughout the industry, individuals with proprietary knowledge move easily between firms, taking competitive advantages with them in their heads.

- **Legalization:** The combination of free agency, depersonalization, and commoditization has created many opportunities for lawyers to get involved with financial services. This legal participation has taken three main forms: individual consumers suing financial companies and advisors, corporate executives protecting themselves and their corporations against lawsuits by demanding greater compliance from their advisors, and industry regulators protecting the main corporations by restricting the activities of innovative advisors.

The case for Unique Process Advisors. Against this industry backdrop, the importance of having a Unique Process is clear to advisors who seek greater control over their professional futures. The biggest problem that all product-based advisors face is that they have no ownership of the intellectual property they sell. Again, it's important to remember that where there is no ownership, there is little or no possibility for greater freedom. Everyone who understands the industry knows that control and power lie in the creation of new Unique Processes that satisfy consumer needs. This is how the industry was created in the first place. This is how the companies in the industry had their start. This is where competitive advantage within the industry has always been found, and this will always be the case in the future. So it makes great sense for financial advisors who want to grow continually in the years and decades ahead to create their own Unique Processes.

***To create and operate from within your own Unique Process,
you have to own your own intellectual property.***

It's important to point out here that financial advisors who create their own
Unique Processes have far more in common with the innovative entrepreneurs
who started and built the financial services industry over the past hundred years
than do the corporate bureaucrats who manage financial corporations today.

A Unique Process is created by combining your own problem-solving wisdom and your clientele's D.O.S.

One of the impacts of microtechnology, as mentioned above, is depersonalization. There is a widening gulf between financial services companies and their
customers. It is this gulf — this absence of personal relationship — that provides the opportunity for creating Unique Processes in the 21st-century marketplace. The three examples of Dan Taylor, Mary Anne Ehlert, and Chuck
Brewster all demonstrate how successful financial advisors, through their
processes, can provide customized and personalized experiences that companies cannot provide. Nor can these personalized experiences be provided by the
product-based advisors who are affiliated with these companies. The transformative experiences provided in these three Unique Processes are clear examples of what sociologist Shoshana Zuboff calls "deep support." In her book,
The Support Economy, co-authored with James Maxmin, Professor Zuboff
describes the growing "disconnect" between large corporations and consumers
in every industry.[10] Her explanation for this disconnect is that:

*Over the past quarter century, individual clients and customers have
changed dramatically in what they want in the way of products, services,
and experiences from large corporations — but large corporations for the
most part have not responded.*

The "Corporate Disability." The very nature of corporations — from
their inception at the beginning of industrialization to the present day — is
to treat individuals in the marketplace as economic children. In other words,

to treat them as passive buyers of mass-produced products and services. The corporations see themselves as powers that be, providing good things to the masses below. They treat their customers that way, and the same top-down attitudes also characterize the way they treat people within their own organizations. As soon as individuals begin moving toward economic adulthood, demanding greater control over their lives and their work, they become incomprehensible to the people running most corporations.

Corporations cannot respond easily or effectively to The Great Crossover because it is generally not within the capability of corporations to deal with individuals as individuals. I call this lack of capability with regard to individuals Corporate Disability, and I believe it exists for the following three reasons.

- **Opposing culture:** The increased freedom from dependency, anxiety, and complexity that large numbers of individuals are seeking in their 21st-century lives runs counter to the culture of most financial corporations, which are characterized by dependency, anxiety, and complexity.

- **Issues too complex:** The emerging issues related to economic adulthood in a microchip-based world are far too complex and fast-changing for any corporation to comprehend.

- **Special focus impossible:** Consumers are ready and willing to pay significant sums for personalized experiences, which are both financially and practically impossible for large corporations to provide.

Incapable of developing meaningful client relationships. The most important implication of this corporate disability is that the majority of large organizations are simply incapable of developing any meaningful relationships with clientele. Bureaucratic managers have very little personal interaction with clients, and are in no position to provide the "deep support" that consumers are looking for. They put an enormous amount of energy into developing and marketing their proprietary products, but rarely have they actually been in a sales situation or sold something successfully. For that reason, they have no conception of what it takes to get someone to write you a cheque.

This chasm between bureaucratic managers and clients creates enormous opportunities for entrepreneurial advisors. Because they are constantly engaged in intimate conversations with clients, advisors are in an extraordinary position to establish powerful client relationships. But only individual financial advisors with Unique Processes are in a position to provide the kind of deep support that increasing numbers of consumers are seeking. The transformation from merely selling products to providing deep support is one that every Unique Process Advisor makes. It begins by having a different kind of conversation about the future with clients and prospects.

The D.O.S. Conversation™.

Professor Zuboff in *The Support Economy* identifies what the best and most affluent consumers in every marketplace are looking for: psychological self-determination. What she means by this is control over their future — all aspects of their future. Yet it is remarkable how infrequently meaningful discussion about the future actually takes place in an industry where many advisors are pressured to focus on the latest product sale and the short-term performance of the market.

From working with thousands of financial advisors over the years, we have identified three factors that always lead to a greater sense of control, to an increased sense of psychological self-determination. These factors are a crucial part of the foundation for every Unique Process that has been created within The Strategic Coach Program. They are also the foundation for financial advisors to create and own their own intellectual property.

Fear, excitement, and confidence. The factors we're talking about are D.O.S., which stands for Dangers, Opportunities, and Strengths. All people experience their daily lives in relation to these three factors. There are dangers that scare them. There are opportunities that excite them. And there are personal strengths they have that give them confidence. All of their needs and requirements, both tangible and intangible, are related to these three D.O.S. issues. If you want to know what makes someone tick, you have to become deeply aware of his or her D.O.S., because this is the center of that individual's motivation.

If you are a financial advisor who wants to become uniquely valuable to your clients, you have to establish and cultivate each relationship on the basis of the person's unique D.O.S. issues.

In The Strategic Coach Program, we teach entrepreneurs to develop what we call The D.O.S. Conversation, which starts with The R-Factor Question®. "R" stands for relationship. Before you can sell anything to someone, you must first sell a relationship. If someone doesn't want to have a relationship with you, they won't want to buy anything else from you. We have learned from the experiences of thousands of financial advisors that there are different ways to ask this question, but no advisor should ever leave a first meeting without having asked it. In its most basic form, this is how the question goes:

"If we were having this discussion three years from now, what has to have happened over those three years for you to feel happy about your progress?"

There are several crucial advantages that this question provides to financial advisors:

1. Quickly eliminates all possibilities except "yes." The R-Factor Question immediately eliminates all "maybe" and "no" prospects. By asking The R-Factor Question, financial advisors quickly eliminate all prospects from consideration except those who are looking for a professional relationship that will lead to a fundamental improvement in their situation.

2. Enables prospects to think backward from the future. In answering the question, prospects visualize themselves three years ahead in time. From that future perspective, they can see much more clearly all the fundamental improvements they want to make in their lives. The R-Factor

Question enables them to eliminate all the minor issues and concerns from their present thinking and to focus on the things that have the greatest long-term importance.

3. Automatically establishes a valuable relationship. As prospects are considering and answering the question, they are automatically in a working relationship with the advisor. Useful work is already being done. By answering the question, prospects are already gaining clarity that they didn't have before. Value is being created.

4. Dramatically differentiates the advisor from others. The R-Factor Question immediately and dramatically positions the financial advisor as different from all other salespeople and consultants. The vast majority of advisors in the financial services industry go into prospect meetings talking about themselves, the companies they represent, and their commoditized products. Advisors who use The R-Factor Question never have to do this. Their credentials, credibility, and creativity are immediately established because they don't talk about themselves, but instead focus entirely on the prospects and their futures.

5. Immediately identifies where value can be created. Prospects' answers to The R-Factor Question immediately tell advisors where to focus their knowledge, experience, and skill. What will emerge from these answers are dangers that need to be eliminated, opportunities that need to be captured, and strengths that need to be maximized. The R-Factor Question always opens the door to an individual's most crucial life issues — the ones that worry them, excite them, and give them confidence.

The R-Factor Question opens the door to the unlimited universe of creating intellectual property.

When financial advisors master The R-Factor Question, their professional lives immediately change for the better. Before using The R-Factor Question, advisors live in a world where they are dependent upon commodities, where they are limited and trapped by bureaucracies and regulators. The first time they use The R-Factor Question effectively, they enter into a world where their professional future depends entirely upon their wisdom and creativity. This is because the R-Factor answers immediately begin the process of developing and owning intellectual property. One financial advisor who was initially skeptical of the impact of the question put it this way:

"The prospect looked at me strangely for a few seconds, but then started to talk. He talked and talked about what was bothering him, both in his business and his personal life. The more he talked, the more emotional he became. The fears were real fears. The things he was excited about were very obvious. And there were a great number of achievements that he was proud of that he didn't want to lose. Based on my experience of solving other people's problems over 17 years, it was very clear how I could be useful. I had knowledge, resources, and skills that he needed, and here he was, laying out a blueprint for me to provide them. I was so amazed by the response, I had to concentrate to keep my mind from wandering to my own possibilities. When our conversation ended an hour later, he wanted to know how soon we could get started.

Driving back to the office, I realized that this was the way the rest of my life could be. Just having great conversations in which the prospects sold themselves on working with me."

Career transformation. Thousands of other financial advisors who are using The R-Factor Question report similar experiences, and a similar sense of career transformation. The biggest realization they come to involves their sense of freedom from financial products, bureaucratic corporations, and regulatory agencies. Until they used The R-Factor Question, they thought the most important factors determining their career were the increasingly commoditized products they had available to sell, their contract with increasingly bureaucratized financial companies, and, of course, being more tightly regulated. The R-Factor Question dramatically changes the look of that future.

But The R-Factor Question is just the beginning. The next step to The D.O.S. Conversation is to determine prospects' key D.O.S. issues. In The Strategic Coach, we do this with the use of a D.O.S. Worksheet™. This is a deceptively simple form that has enormous impact on the thinking of both prospects and advisors. Within the same conversation that was opened with The R-Factor Question, advisors begin to zero in on the most important dangers, opportunities, and strengths prospects have. Here's how the conversation goes:

"Based on what you've just told me about what has to happen over the next three years, what are the biggest dangers (or problems, worries, or concerns) that need to be eliminated?"

Now that the prospects are thinking within this three-year framework, they usually respond with a list of worrisome issues. Advisors, as they are listening to this, make notes. When the list seems complete, the advisors read back what they've written. Here, again, this represents information that is very valuable to the prospects. When they hear the list, they may change the wording or add other items. But when the list seems satisfactory, the advisors next ask:

"Of these items, which are the top three? In what order of priority?"

Advisors who use The D.O.S. Conversation regularly say that, by this time in the discussion, the prospects have bought into the working relationship. They see the advisor as someone who is already useful, and can be even more so. Once the three most important dangers are identified, the same process is used to identify the most important opportunities:

"For you to be happy with your progress over the next three years, what are the most important opportunities that need to be captured?"

Again the advisors compile a list as the prospects talk, and then work to narrow it down to the three most important items. One of the things that makes The

D.O.S. Conversation work most effectively is the practice of repeating back to prospects what they have said, and asking if they want to clarify or add anything. The final step is to identify the prospects' strengths:

"Over the next three years, what are the most important strengths that you already have, both business and personal, that need to be captured?"

Strengths are a source of crucial confidence. These last issues are very important to the development of the relationship because they are a source of confidence to the prospects. People can understand their dangers and opportunities very clearly, but they lack the personal confidence to do anything about them. Without confidence, they can't make decisions. Without confidence, they can't take action. The term "strengths" relates to achievements, capabilities, and resources that the prospects already have in hand. For the most part, they will not think about these until they are brought to their attention. But once they are, people immediately become more confident and committed to move forward.

With The D.O.S. Worksheet completed, advisors now go back over the nine crucial issues: three dangers, three opportunities, and three strengths. Although the responses of prospects to The D.O.S. Conversation vary enormously, the financial advisors we work with in The Strategic Coach report several that seem to be common.

- **Transformation:** After going through The D.O.S. Conversation, prospects are visibly changed from when the meeting began. They are more upbeat, enthusiastic, and focused. They are confident where they used to be worried and anxious. Our interpretation of this feedback is that The D.O.S. Conversation has dramatically raised their Ceiling of Complexity. What seemed confusing and paralyzing now seems simple and energizing. They've gained an invaluable amount of personal clarity about how the various dimensions in their life are working for and against each other.

- **Commitment:** In a very short time (usually not more than an hour), the prospect has gained sufficient reason to commit themselves to a working relationship with the advisor. When they arrived at the meeting, they probably expected yet another product pitch. Instead, they finally found an advisor willing to listen and discuss the things that really matter in their life. Most people have never had an opportunity to talk about their dangers, opportunities, and strengths in such an upfront manner. No one else — none of their other colleagues, associates, advisors, or friends — has ever enabled them to see things so clearly, so comprehensively, and so quickly.

- **Partnership:** The process of The D.O.S. Conversation requires that prospects and advisors act as partners to create a vision of the future. There is no superior or inferior here. The prospects contribute the content of the conversation, and the advisors contribute the structure for identifying priorities and making clear choices. This partnership will remain in place for the duration of the relationship, however long it lasts.

- **Urgency:** With the key issues in their life now clear, prospects want to move forward to solutions as quickly as possible. They realize that financial advisors cannot provide the entire solution — because many issues will require the expertise of other kinds of specialists. But clients now know that financial advisors are the central players, the ones who helped to clarify the "big picture." Just by allowing clients to have this conversation and think within this framework, you are automatically providing them with far more value than they have ever received from any financial advisor — or any other advisor in their life.

Completed D.O.S. Conversations are an endless source of building blocks for creating intellectual property.

The only way that leads to freedom. Having worked with thousands of financial advisors, I feel confident in stating that The D.O.S. Conversation is the only sure-fire way for financial advisors to create intellectual property that will continually increase their freedom of time, money, relationship, and purpose. Other advisors who try to create intellectual property invariably run into obstacles and frustrations that defeat their efforts to achieve greater personal and professional freedom. Each completed D.O.S. Conversation represents building blocks for creating intellectual property that an advisor can truly own. The D.O.S. Conversation is just the first stage, but without it, it is difficult to make any other kind of breakthroughs. There are just too many forces of complexity, bureaucracy, and regulation at work within the financial services industry for advisors to make creative headway without the clarity and protection that The D.O.S. Conversation provides each time that it's used.

The packaging stage. As powerful as The D.O.S. Conversation is, it is just raw material. The next stage is to transform the initial information revealed by the conversation into a conceptual framework that becomes a complete problem-solving process for the specific prospect — and also a template for approaching other prospects. In The Strategic Coach, we call this next stage "packaging." It means taking raw information and developing it into a form that impacts prospects in a positive, appealing, and memorable way. In the world at large, the most successful examples of intellectual property are the ones that have superior packaging. Let's see what this means for financial advisors.

Freedom 2:
Packaging Client Breakthroughs

One of the things The D.O.S. Conversation does immediately for financial advisors is free them from their dependence on financial products and companies. The reason for this is simple: The entire conversation takes place without advisors ever having to talk about products or companies. When this first occurs, advisors are amazed. Here is what one experienced advisor reported:

"From day one of my career (as a life insurance agent), I'd been told to talk in glowing terms about the company I represented and the superior products that we offered. All my sales training was geared toward showing how we were so much better than the other companies and their products. But in The D.O.S. Conversation, I didn't have to mention this at all. The prospect didn't ask about companies and products, and I couldn't see any point in bringing up the subject. In fact, looking back, if I had said anything along those lines, it would have ruined the conversation. The conversation was about him, not me. As a matter of fact, I didn't say very much about myself at all. The whole focus was on him. And that's why it worked so well."

Consumers don't care, and don't want to know. Financial services corporations, which are in the business of creating and marketing commodities, spend billions of dollars trying to convince financial advisors and their clientele how important those commodities are. But The D.O.S. Conversation reveals a fundamental truth: Consumers have little or no interest in knowing very much about these commodities or about the corporations that market them. What they are really interested in is their own futures, especially the things that are going to make those futures better. People have things that worry them, that excite them, and that make them feel confident — and these are the only things they really want to talk about. And virtually all consumers in today's marketplace know that no large corporation is interested in them as individuals. No matter what the advertising says, they know that no one in some faraway head office will ever take a personal interest in their individual welfare and progress. Many also know there is nothing that any large financial corporation can mass produce that will provide them with the specific solutions they're looking for.

The D.O.S. Conversation enables advisors and prospects — as creative partners — to bypass the whole subject of financial products and companies.

Going back to our discussion of "freedom from" and "freedom to," it's clear how The D.O.S. Conversation provides both possibilities.

- **Freedom from:** Advisors are permanently freed from having to talk about anything related to the financial services industry. By not talking about products, services, or companies, they immediately differentiate themselves from competitors, who can't talk about anything else. They are permanently freed from being associated in prospects' minds with any kind of commodity.

- **Freedom to:** Advisors are permanently freed to focus entirely on being valuable and useful in ways that their clients most want and need. The universe of emerging D.O.S. issues — as we will demonstrate — is infinite, and so are the new ways of being useful and valuable. The more advisors utilize The D.O.S. Conversation, the more capable they become as independent problem-solvers in the marketplace.

Packaging the D.O.S. issues. The D.O.S. Conversation, then, represents a first stage of achieving advisor freedom throughout the 21st century. But it's just the first stage, and many more are possible. The next stage involves "packaging" the raw material of the client or prospect's D.O.S. issues with the advisor's wisdom to create a process that can be bought. We live in a world that is filled with every kind of packaging, but as it relates to financial advisors in the 21st century, we mean the following.

- **Direction:** Providing prospects and clients with extraordinary and lasting clarity about their future, based on an evolving gameplan that transforms their unique D.O.S. issues into fundamental and lasting solutions.

- **Confidence:** Providing clientele with a sense of extraordinary and lasting relationship — one that continually contributes to a growing sense of confidence that the future will always be better.

- **Capability:** Providing clientele with extraordinary and lasting concepts and tools for thinking strategically about all aspects of their lives — then for making decisions and taking actions that always produce better results.

These three factors relate back to the issues of confusion, isolation, and powerlessness that were discussed in the Opportunity section. The biggest impact of unpredictable change in a microchip-based world is that it undermines direction, confidence, and capability. Without these three things, individuals are unable to think clearly, make good decisions, or take effective actions. Hence, they remain trapped in dependency, anxiety, and complexity.

All specific solutions in the financial services industry in the 21st century — if they are to be effective and lasting — must be packaged with direction, confidence, and capability.

Anytime these three factors are present, prospects and clients immediately have a sense that value is being created for them. The D.O.S. Conversation, consisting of The R-Factor Question and The D.O.S. Worksheet, already provides value in a unique fashion. The next action for financial advisors, after they have discovered a prospect's crucial D.O.S. issues, is to package these in a document that makes the creative relationship official.

The D.O.S. Letter serves as the permanent "package" for cultivating the relationship between clients and advisors.

In order to maximize the positive impact and progress achieved in The D.O.S. Conversation, advisors next send a letter to the prospect as soon as possible. This is a very specific and strategic letter. We call it The D.O.S. Letter, and it has three main components:

1. Reiteration. The advisors reflect back, in writing, the prospects' most important three-year goals and the nine key D.O.S. issues. One of the interesting impacts of this reiteration is that the prospects are typically amazed by the information. Most of them don't remember having said these things and are deeply impressed by the advisors' "intuitive" grasp of their situation. At the very least, they are impressed by how well the advisors listened. Upon reading what was recorded in the initial meeting, they are even more deeply committed to moving forward on these issues and their solutions.

2. Credibility, credentials, and creativity. This is the point where the advisors state something about themselves. It includes three things in particular. First, an initial plan of action that will begin transforming the prospects' issues into solutions. Second, a brief account of the advisors' credentials and experiences in creating these types of solutions. And, third, specific tools and processes the advisors have created to produce these solutions. We have discovered from the experience of hundreds of advisors that the briefer and more understated this second section is, the better.

The fact that the advisors have a thorough grasp of their clients' issues is the best way that they can impress their prospects.

Prospects want to know what the advisor has in mind as an approach, what they've done in the past, and what kind of unique tools they have — but not much more.

3. Three specific actions. The advisors end The D.O.S. Letter by outlining three specific actions that will begin the problem-solving process. One of these three actions is to send an invoice so that the prospects can write a cheque. All the work that's been done to this point, including The R-Factor Question, The D.O.S. Worksheet, and now The D.O.S. Letter, represents a significant contribution and commitment on the part of the advisors. Now it's time for the prospects to make a commitment, thereby becoming clients. One of two things will happen: The prospects will either write a cheque or not. If they do, the advisors have a client; if not, they immediately move on to someone else. The important thing is for them not to do any more work until they receive payment.

By packaging your client relationships, you permanently remove them from competition and commoditization.

A financial advisor in Australia was having trouble getting commitments from his prospects, who were mostly physicians. He had very good referrals, but after an initial meeting with these prospects, it was difficult to set up second meetings.

As soon as he began using The D.O.S. Conversation as his first meeting — and then following up with The D.O.S. Letter — he made 56 sales in a row, all of them within two months of starting the relationship.

In fact, he was so successful, he had to suspend his efforts for a while for his staff to catch up with the paperwork. Although this is the most dramatic example we can cite, virtually all the other advisors who use this approach report a big jump in their closing rates. But the whole issue here is more than just getting a sale; what the D.O.S. approach enables advisors to do is to establish long-term relationships with the very best clients. By "very best" we mean that the relationships keep getting better, both in terms of significant progress for the clients and high profitability for the advisors. These high-quality relationships have a number of benefits that play a significant role in transforming the advisor's future. Here are some of the advantages that the D.O.S. approach, as a form of packaging, provides.

- **A strategic partnership based on equal commitment:** The vast majority of financial advisors in the industry are always at a serious disadvantage in their relationships with their clientele. They have to make an enormous upfront commitment in terms of time, effort, expertise, and out-of-pocket expense before the prospect or client commits anything except a small amount of time. It is not unusual for advisors to devote six months of work before being paid anything. Too often, they invest that amount of effort and get paid nothing. The reason for this, of course, is that they are selling a commodity. All of their wisdom, experience, and unique capabilities are just so much added value.

  In the D.O.S. approach, the advisors never go more than a week or so into a relationship before receiving a cheque. And, as we will show, there are continual requirements throughout the process for the clients to deepen their commitment to the partnership. This continually increasing commitment on the part of clientele is the biggest guarantee that the relationship will be long-lasting and transformative.

- **Protection against commodity-based advisors:** One thing all of the advisors who use D.O.S. to package their relationships comment on is that they have become immune to competition. It happens so quickly, it usually takes them by surprise. When you're in the marketplace selling commodities, you always have to worry about other advisors selling similar kinds of products that offer superior features or lower prices, or both. Many successful advisors say they never worry about this — until they lose an important client relationship, or until they notice that it's getting more difficult to sell the commodities. Then they worry a lot. Advisors who use the D.O.S. approach never worry about commodities at all. The reason is that the commodities — financial products and services — are all relegated to the status of "tools for implementation." Most of the advisors in The Strategic Coach Program report that within their D.O.S.-packaged relationships, the subject of which products to use to implement their solutions either doesn't come up at all as a topic of discussion, or only arises very late in the strategic process.

- **Process fees eliminate dependence on commissions:** Commodity-based advisors are entirely dependent on the commissions they receive from the sale of products. The size of these commissions is determined by the financial corporations and therefore can be reduced arbitrarily. Some commodity advisors think they have gotten around their dependence on commissions by switching to receiving fees based on the amount of assets under management. But these "fees" are still commissions under another name, and subject to the same unpredictability. The case with D.O.S.-based advisors is starkly different. They receive fees for their unique wisdom, experience, and capabilities that have nothing to do with the sale of commodities. And, they still receive commissions when they sell products. Over a period of time, the process fees can match and exceed the amount of money each year they make from commissions and asset management fees.

A growing number of D.O.S.-based advisors have become so accomplished in packaging their client relationships that they forego commodity-based sales altogether. They farm this part of the implementation process out to other advisors, which means that at a certain point, they no longer need their industry licenses. They may relinquish them or keep them, but the point is that they no longer depend upon them to make an increasingly good living. They become free of bureaucratic and regulatory oversight, control, and interference.

- **Future determined by clientele rather than industry:** Most financial advisors at the present time need an all-encompassing structure of industry protections in order to make a living. By this I mean they need a business card that says they officially represent some well-known corporation. They need to have letters after their name that say they have achieved certain kinds of professional credentials and licenses. They need to have financial products produced and packaged by others in order to have something to sell. And they need to be part of a successful marketing organization where a manager directs and motivates them on a continual basis and provides administrative processing for all of the business they do. All advisors probably need all or part of this support at the beginning of their careers, but some need it on a permanent basis. For those who need it permanently, their future is forever determined and controlled by the industry. They are truly and completely captive. Without the support structures listed above, they wouldn't know how to make money. As competitors in the marketplace, they wouldn't know what to say. Without all of these things backing them up, they wouldn't know how to think about their professional futures.

No need. Those who become skillful with the D.O.S.-based process quickly find that they don't need any of these industry-based supports in order to create success, satisfaction, and significance in their client relationships. Each new successful sale of their process to a client enables them to free themselves more from industry dependence. *Instead of looking to the financial industry for their career protection, they now look to their clientele.*

Their clients, now trained to think in terms of D.O.S., are always presenting them with new dangers, opportunities, and strengths to transform with their process. And because these advisors continually become more valuable to their best clients, they are continually referred to new prospects of equal or greater quality.

• **Little risk of lawsuit:** Unique Process Advisors operating within a D.O.S. approach rarely have to worry about being sued by their clients. That's because they develop such strong relationships with clients. The D.O.S. Conversation provides advisors with extraordinary clarity about what matters most to clients, while setting out a clear blueprint for what clients should expect from their advisors. For that reason, it minimizes the potential for conflict. Simply put, from our experience, very few, if any, Unique Process Advisors have ever been the target of a client lawsuit.

How the possibilities offered by a Unique Process transform the thinking of commodity-based advisors.

The D.O.S. process we have described so far secures a client relationship. However, in order to keep and grow that relationship, something different, which I call a Unique Process, is required. Before describing how a Unique Process is developed, I need to point out something very important:

Virtually every experienced financial advisor I have met over the past 35 years has a Unique Process.

By this I mean that he or she has developed a unique "pattern" of thinking, communication, problem-solving, and implementation that leads to results for the clientele and to a paycheque. This pattern has been continually improved and refined through thousands of hours of trial and error. The pattern combines insights about human nature in general, about the clients in particular, as well as in-depth knowledge about financial products and services, the economy, the stock market, and various aspects of accounting and law. All of this has been combined, through the experience of thousands of prospect presentations and client relationships, into a cohesive set of effective strategies. This pattern, from our standpoint, is a Unique Process — not a complete one, not a conscious one, but one that can serve as the foundation for 80 percent of what is needed to design and package a Unique Process that stands on its own in the marketplace.

When I sit down with a veteran advisor, I can immediately see the structure of their Unique Process starting to emerge. I can see it, but they can't. Where I see each of the stages, they just see an automatic series of activities that has been refined through constant trial and error.

Nothing is organized. Nothing is written down. Nothing is packaged. And nothing is communicated to clients. Regardless of how much wisdom an advisor puts into his process, he essentially shields this wisdom from clients by never giving them a true sense of all the value being created in the relationship.

I speak to a lot of advisor audiences. When I point out to them that they already have a Unique Process, as I have described it above, many of them nod in agreement. They know what I'm talking about. They know that they have a process that has developed over many years, a process that makes them confident and successful. But from their perspective, this process is only designed to sell commodities. As soon as they begin to see that their process also has unique, separate value in the eyes of prospects and clients, they are dumbstruck.

This single moment of realization completely transforms their understanding of their financial careers. Here's how I characterize this transformation of thinking — and imagination.

- **Everything they've done to this point is R & D:** If they've been working in the marketplace for 15 or 20 years, they now realize that all of it was simply for the purpose of preparation. The successes, the failures, and the long hours of work were all to learn about what works and what doesn't in establishing, building, and keeping client relationships. Everything they've done until now has a profound meaning — as research and development for the next stage of their career.

- **Selling products was just training for something much bigger and better:** All entrepreneurs in all industries start their careers by selling products of some sort to particular kinds of clients. There is no other way to gain crucial marketplace experience. There is no other way to understand how, why, and when people write cheques. And there is no other way to learn how to see the world from the buyers' standpoint. In the financial services industry, this experience of selling products is necessary training, first for developing a Unique Process, and then for designing a way to have that Unique Process pay for itself — with or without a product to go along with it.

- **Everything they dislike about the industry can be quickly bypassed within their own Unique Process:** I meet and talk with thousands of financial advisors every year who are still commodity-dependent. When it comes to the frustrations, annoyances, and grievances they experience within the financial services industry, they have very long lists — too long and tedious to itemize in this book. And, besides, there is no need to dwell on these negative factors: The Unique Process bypasses most of them very quickly.

Virtually everything disagreeable about being a financial advisor in the 21st century is attributable to being dependent on the sale of products. Once advisors free themselves from this dependency by operating from within their own Unique Process, most of the frustrations quickly disappear and never come back.

- **The Unique Process allows advisors to experience extraordinary profit growth:** Many advisors are reluctant to "rock the boat" and give up their dependency on product sales, because they continue to earn a generous income. Even the most captive and commoditized advisors can make over $1 million if they're gifted salespeople. Few other professions offer this kind of earning potential. In these circumstances, many captive advisors will put up with all the hassles because they believe that "things are as good as they can get." These advisors are entirely concerned with preserving the status quo and protecting what they have, rather than creating a bigger future for their business.

Yet if it comes down to a raw financial calculation, this career decision should be easy: The long-term earning potential of a Unique Process Advisor is exponentially greater than that of any captive advisor. If you're currently a high-income advisor, then you are precisely the kind of advisor with the capabilities, opportunities, and resources to experience huge growth with a Unique Process. Top producers who reluctantly tolerate growing bureaucratic restrictions in order to maintain their income actually have the most to lose by staying captive.

At The Strategic Coach, we've seen countless examples of entrepreneurs who have shifted to a Unique Process and never looked back. On the following pages, you'll read what a few of them told us:

"Both my revenues and profits have increased by at least six times since I started the Unique Process. What's interesting is that right now I don't even see that as a big deal. I'm just scratching the surface of what's possible in the years ahead."

Another advisor said:

"My revenues and profits are now easily ten times what they were a few years ago, and they are predictable, where my product-based income wasn't. My company now has a real value, probably a five-times multiplier of my earnings. That would have never happened if I had continued to rely on product sales. What's even better, I feel that we are just getting started. The sky's the limit."

In my position as a coach to many of these Unique Process Advisors, I've witnessed first-hand how rapid and explosive the growth can be. Indeed, I've seen many Unique Process Advisors who have been paid tens of thousands of dollars simply for asking a number of extraordinarily effective questions. I've seen incredibly powerful multimedia presentations that were put together in a matter of days, but that ended up netting hundreds of thousands of dollars.

- **Every professional goal, ideal, and value can be realized through the Unique Process:** Probably the biggest surprise that advisors have in operating from within a Unique Process is that it's not just about business. It's not just about freeing themselves from commoditization, bureaucracy, and regulation. It's not just about making a very good living — much better than they ever thought possible. The big surprise is that the Unique Process is about their whole life. It's about everything they've ever wanted to accomplish, everything they've wanted to prove about themselves, and everything they've ever wanted to create and contribute. That's one reason they give up all ideas of retirement. I remember one advisor in his sixties who had almost left the industry before he, fortunately, discovered the Unique Process approach. After a year of this new kind of life, this is what he said to me:

"I feel like I'm just starting over again, but at an incredibly higher level. I have the same excitement and enthusiasm as in the first years, only now I also have this extraordinary set of opportunities and capa-

bilities available to me. I was so exhausted and frustrated before making the change. I would have left before I was sixty-five. Now I want to work till ninety. Longer, if I can."

There is a reason for this renewed excitement and motivation:

Financial advisors who operate successfully from within a Unique Process are the most advanced examples of economic adults in the world. Not only have they freed themselves from dependence, anxiety, and complexity, their daily business is helping others do the same thing. This means that on a daily basis, they can live their lives out of their highest ideals and deepest values. The vehicle of the Unique Process enables them to achieve their greatest goals and continually provides them with the most expansive freedoms available to anyone during this century.

These are some of the important realizations that come to commodity-based advisors when they understand how a Unique Process can transform their careers and their lives. They realize that right now they don't have the ability to package their relationships in the manner described in this section. In fact, they clearly realize for the first time that it is they who have been packaged — by the products, and by the bureaucrats and the regulators. Now they know that they have to gain freedom from all these constraints in order to have the freedom to design and live the professional and personal lives they desire.

The next stage: designing, naming, and implementing the Unique Process to create a marketplace monopoly.

In the next section, Freedom 3, we will describe, in the briefest possible form, how the Unique Process is turned into a creative operating vehicle in the marketplace. What we most want for you as a result of your Unique Process is to have a monopoly on the experience you create for your clients. We want you to transform your unique talents as an individual and all of your wisdom, experience, and expertise into a lucrative market niche that is entirely yours for the remainder of your career.

Over 30 years' experience in this area tells us that the greatest breakthroughs in designing, naming, and implementing Unique Processes take place within an ongoing series of creative conversations among like-minded advisors. Spontaneous insights and breakthroughs occur in that kind of setting. Questions are naturally and quickly answered by the participants. Confidence comes from having enthusiastic and courageous companions in the trial-and-error process of mutual learning, growth, and success. While this book can't substitute for that experience, it can serve as a guide by summarizing the best of what we have learned from leading, observing, and participating in these conversations.

Freedom 3:
Achieving An Experience Monopoly

An advisor had created a Unique Process that was producing dramatically improved results for his clientele — and was also producing abnormally high sales of life insurance and investments. The president of a large financial corporation heard about the advisor's success and invited him for a conference with senior management. All of these individuals were enthusiastic about the idea of licensing the Unique Process for all their "captive" advisors. The president was very keen and commented that this was the breakthrough he had been looking for, and that he couldn't wait to have the Unique Process working throughout the system. "Of course," he said, "we'll have to see what our compliance department says." The advisor, who had already been through this routine with several other corporations, responded:

"Oh, I'm sorry. I thought you were the president of this company. I thought you made the decisions. If your lawyers are actually the ones making policy here, I should have gone straight to them."

The president was embarrassed and said that it was simply a formality. But, of course, it wasn't. The head compliance lawyer didn't like the idea, and that was the end of it. President or no president, the lawyers were the ones who were actually running the corporation.

Intellectual and creative bankruptcy. Over the past ten years, I have listened to thousands of stories from financial advisors describing how they are losing their professional freedom within an industry that is increasingly governed and directed by lawyers. The legal control of the industry comes in three forms: plaintiff lawyers who launch lawsuits against individual advisors, regulators who continually burden advisors with prohibitions, and corporate compliance lawyers who continually restrict the ability of advisors to differentiate themselves in the marketplace. All of this legal interference into advisors' daily lives simply points to the intellectual and creative bankruptcy of most corporate head offices. *The vast majority of executives and managers in financial corporations are still trying to operate 20th-century industrial organizations in a 21st-century consumer environment.*

Out-of-touch management, ambitious lawyers. With each passing quarter, corporate management grows farther out of touch with the emerging D.O.S. issues of financial clients and customers. Bureaucrats at head offices are incapable of having the kind of in-depth D.O.S. Conversations that would tell them what clients actually want in the way of financial direction, confidence, and capability. This out-of-touch quality represents a fundamental breakdown of relationship with the buying public, which opens the door for tens of thousands of lawyers to move in to key decision-making roles. Since the executives and managers are increasingly ignorant about what clients actually want, they need growing ranks of lawyers to protect them from making serious errors of judgement and execution that could damage their organizations' reputation and viability — and their own careers.

Viewed from this perspective, what is currently occurring is a de facto takeover of the financial services industry by the legal industry. Whenever I speak about this development to audiences of financial advisors, I always receive applause. Based on what has already been happening, it is possible to predict how this takeover will progress over the next decade.

- **Regulators will dictate corporate strategy:** Increasingly, senior management at financial corporations will consult with regulators before developing new products and services, marketing strategies, and campaigns.

- **Compliance will control marketing and sales:** Within financial corporations, the heads of marketing and sales will report to the head of compliance — and will only communicate and implement as directed by the latter.

- **Lawyers will become senior management:** Increasingly, the positions of C.E.O. and president in financial corporations will be filled by corporate and regulatory lawyers.

- **Corporations will use regulation to eliminate independent organizations and advisors:** Increasingly, financial corporations will encourage greater regulation and compliance in order to increase the legal restrictions and costs faced by independent marketing organizations and advisors — thereby eliminating their creative advantages and profit margins.

Can't be reversed. Every quarter, I receive dozens of head office memos, pronouncements from regulatory bodies, and industry publications that give solid evidence that these trends are speeding up. My sense is that for financial advisors who remain dependent on bureaucratic organizations and on commoditized products, the situation can only grow worse. For independent advisors whose livelihood also depends entirely on the sale of products, the future will become more unpredictable, complicated, onerous, and precarious. The legal takeover of financial services is now so far advanced at the corporate level that there is no possibility of it being reversed. Once lawyers get a firm hold of any situation, it's very difficult to remove them, or even lessen their influence. It's important for entrepreneurially-minded advisors to realize this, because an extraordinary strategy is required to escape from the legal snares and traps being planned and set for them. Fortunately, advisors who are developing and expanding their own Unique Processes are blazing the trail for others in this respect.

The best way to bypass legalization is to create a Unique Process that becomes a marketplace monopoly.

In the overview to this Freedom section, I cited the examples of three advisors who have created their own Unique Processes. I am going to focus on one of them, Mary Anne Ehlert, to demonstrate in practical terms how a D.O.S. Conversation becomes an actual problem-solving process. Mary Anne started off in the banking industry, then became an investment advisor. Over a 15-year career, she began noticing that she had a special interest and special abilities in dealing with families with a special-needs individual. This could be either a child, a spouse, or a parent who was disabled in some way. Mary Anne had a sister with special needs, so she knew first-hand the difficult pressures this situation places on all members of a family. Mary Anne also noticed that all the institutions in society, including political and social institutions, that are supposed to provide guidance and support to families with special needs, don't.

Institutions, whether government, corporate, or non-profit, are invariably bureaucracies, and bureaucrats, when they are useful at all, are only good at dealing with problems in a general sense.

They usually fail when it comes to dealing with the needs and issues of specific individuals. This, of course, is where financial advisors shine — especially advisors who are skilled at conducting The D.O.S. Conversation.

Huge vacuum that needed filling. What Mary Anne Ehlert discovered in the process of conducting many D.O.S. Conversations was that most of the serious issues of special-needs families were largely or entirely unmet or ignored by the institutions that were supposed to address them. In other words, there was a huge vacuum in society where knowledge and skill were supposed to be. In the United States, this creates a very big problem, since over ten percent of all families have a family member with special needs. Reflecting on this entire situation, Mary Anne, as an entrepreneur, decided to create a fundamental solution in the marketplace. Her many D.O.S. Conversations revealed the following set of issues.

- **Parents and children overwhelmed:** Families with special needs are overwhelmed by the experience. Neither the parents nor the children in these families are able to lead normal lives, since everything revolves around the care of the individual with special needs. It's frequently the case that there are no family vacations, and the children are expected to carry responsibilities that limit their normal childhood activities and enjoyments. Mary Anne discovered that this feeling of being overwhelmed was as true for wealthy families as for poor ones. Adding to the sense of overwhelm was the experience of there being no central agency that could supply up-to-date knowledge, resources, and capabilities.

- **The institutions in all fields were ignorant, incompetent, or uncaring:** Mary Anne discovered that, while there are many dedicated and skillful people working in this field, on the whole, the institutions are failing at the job. Again, bureaucracy is the central problem. The people in charge are disconnected from the individuals seeking help. There is a great deal of useful information and knowledge, but it is disorganized and unfocused. Too many managers and employees in the various institutions see their work as simply a job, not as a crucial area of value creation in society. They can't be bothered to do anything more than what their job description — and their career advancement — calls for.

- **The biggest worries were not addressed:** The single biggest worry that income earners in special-needs families have is dying before the person with special needs does. They also fear that, if their income were to decrease, or their savings were to become depleted, they would lose control over the situation. They don't know what would happen to their family member — child, spouse, or parent — if they weren't around.

- **There was no financial planning or plan:** Institutions have failed to address the central issues of financial strategy, implementation, and management. Government bureaucrats lack the skills, knowledge, and experience to help in this area — as do social workers. The educational system and the legal system, as well, provide no guidance to the families in the crucial endeavor of underwriting the support that the person with special needs requires for his or her entire lifetime.

- **No one was in charge:** What may be the biggest problem for special-needs families is that there are no "quarterbacks" — no single individuals with the knowledge, skill, influence, and commitment to provide long-range support to the families and to the family member with special needs.

Perfect opportunities. Mary Anne Ehlert is dealing with a specific problem in modern society, but there are thousands of situations like hers. One of the main impacts of the microchip revolution is what I call "The Bureaucratic Breakdown." Without going too deeply into historical analysis, it is safe to say that bureaucracy as we know it today is almost entirely a development of the Industrial Age. The creation of massive industrial processes — and the necessity of dealing with the affairs of masses of industrial workers — called for top-down organizational structures where things could be done in predictable, standardized, impersonal ways. For most of the 19th and 20th centuries, this was a fairly effective approach, but now almost all bureaucracies are failing.

People living in modern societies now want specialized, custom-designed support for non-predictable issues and concerns. This is something that few, if any, bureaucratic organizations can comprehend — let alone respond to in a satisfying manner. What this means is that there is a huge area of opportunity opening up for entrepreneurs.

Wherever there is bureaucratic failure, there is an opportunity for entrepreneurs with a Unique Process.

Mary Anne Ehlert clearly saw the opportunity and created a Unique Process to fill the vacuum. She transformed the five problem areas listed previously into practice strategies, solutions, and systems that are now having a major impact on the lives of thousands of American families. Starting as a single individual with an insight into a new form of value creation in the marketplace, Mary Anne has now created a dynamic and growing organization that is increasingly recognized as the central problem-solver in the area of families with special needs. What's important to reiterate is that she was able to create her Unique Process because of her training, experience, and success as a financial advisor. No other specialist could have created the solution. It is the combination of financial expertise, on the one hand, and her grasp of human psychology, on the other, that enabled Mary Anne to design a system of strategies and solutions that works better than anything else in American society. Let's look at what these strategies and solutions are, and how Mary Anne organized them into her Unique Process.

Organization that provides profound experience. First of all, it's important to realize that a Unique Process, as we teach this concept and capability in The Strategic Coach Program, is *a set of organized, integrated actions that provide clients with a profound sense of direction, confidence, and capability — where all of these things were previously missing.* In Mary Anne Ehlert's approach, this set of actions looks like the following — with each stage of action, there is practical progress, and a positive emotional impact:

1. Take a Candid Look* (Identification of needs). This provides the families with an honest appraisal of their situation, and what will be required to make it better. *It provides them with the relief of knowing the truth, and knowing that they are not alone.*

2. Create the Future Map* (Life plan). This stage provides the family with direction for the future, and a step-by-step process for increasing protection for the individual with special needs. *The biggest emotional value here is that, perhaps for the first time, families have hope that things will get better.*

3. Filter the Legal Options* (Estate plan with attorney). This is a deeper stage of financial planning, where all family and financial eventualities and contingencies are taken into account — and legal structures are provided to guarantee the implementation of effective actions. *Now, again for the first time, the family feels that it has an organized long-range structure for thinking, communicating, and acting.*

4. Capture Potential Benefits* (Application for government benefits). The various governments — federal, state, county, and municipal — have a wide range of benefits for families in these situations, but because of bureaucracy, they are not easy to learn about or access. This part of the process identifies the maximum benefits that are possible for the family, and then sets in motion the steps to secure them. *Families are usually extremely grateful for this help in dealing with institutions that are so often uncaring and unresponsive.*

5. Document the Wonder* (History of family member documented). A multi-dimensional biography and profile of the person with special needs is created that clearly demonstrates that he or she is a unique individual. Everything the individual needs on a personal level is documented. *This stage creates positive and supportive attitudes in everyone — including the family members — so the individual can always be provided with comfortable and caring support.*

6. Begin the Transition* (Residential, employment, and recreation research). One of the most important contingencies to prepare for is the person with special needs living outside of the family home. *Again, knowing where to look and how to judge one program from another is a headache for special-needs families. When this is organized for them, they have enormous peace of mind. In time, they get to lead normal lives again.*

7. Fund the Future* (Asset analysis). When everything is in place, the entire process is underwritten and secured with proper financial solutions. *For the first time, many families have financial peace of mind. Everything has been anticipated, everything has been planned, and everything has been implemented.*

8. Review and Renew* (Annual assessment). After all the other stages are complete, the future care plan is reviewed on an annual basis in order to accommodate and address life's inevitable changes. *For most special-needs families, this is an overwhelmingly complex process of thinking, decision-making, and implementation. They are very thankful that someone knowledgeable and skillful is handling this for them.*

Beyond bureaucracy. This is a necessarily brief overview of what Mary Anne Ehlert's Process for Protected Tomorrows provides to a growing number of families. It takes only a few moments to realize that the support built into her process is beyond the intellectual comprehension and practical capability of financial bureaucracies. *Only an entrepreneurial financial advisor — with years of personal and professional experience in the problem area — could have designed the multi-dimensional strategies, solutions, and systems of this process.*

By examining just this one example, it's possible to gain insight into how all entrepreneurial advisors with Unique Processes can approach their clientele's issues and concerns. Although each Unique Process Advisor comes from a different starting point with their own unique experience, passion, and commitment, there are common components to how all Unique Processes are created.

- **Everything starts with D.O.S:** All raw material for creating a Unique Process comes from the D.O.S. Conversations conducted with individual prospects and clients.

- **Transform issues into action-strategies:** Every key concern or issue of clientele is transformed into a strategy that will lead to significant improvements and progress.

- **Establish the practical benefits:** How each action-strategy will benefit the client is clearly articulated.

- **Identify the emotional impact:** Each action stage is designed to have a positive and lasting emotional impact on the clientele.

- **Organize actions into a single system:** The action-strategies are all integrated in a sequence that has a beginning, middle, and end. This single system is the Unique Process.

- **Name the stages and the process:** It's important for marketing and differentiation purposes to name each action-strategy and the overall system of actions. The names communicate to clients the benefits of the process and its emotional impact. The skillful use of descriptive language can give enormous meaning to a Unique Process.

- **Illustrate the process with a simple diagram:** For communication purposes, it's crucial to develop a one-page diagram that provides a clear, "at-a-glance" overview of the entire Unique Process.

The power of Unique Processes lies in providing unique value experiences in an increasingly commoditized world.

What I've described so far, obviously, represents a very different way for advisors to approach the marketplace. Instead of selling commoditized products or services, they are offering a unique thinking-and-planning experience. The important word here is "experience." An experience is the opposite of a commodity. As we move further into the 21st century, all of the economic breakthroughs in the global economy are being found increasingly in the area of unique consumer experiences. This can be seen most clearly right now in the hospitality, tourism, and entertainment industries. But the concept of unique experience is quickly taking hold in every other industry. The reason is simple: Individuals will pay a premium for an experience that separates them from being treated like a commodity. As more and more of everyday life is commoditized by large corporations, individuals are increasingly open to unique, memorable, and motivating experiences provided by entrepreneurs in all fields.

Millions looking for breakthroughs. Mary Anne Ehlert's opportunity to create value has been created by the commoditized treatment that families with special needs generally receive from government and corporate bureaucracies. The bureaucracies can't help themselves from doing this: Commodities and commoditization are the only things they know. It's just that millions of individuals no longer want to be treated this way, and are looking for the kinds of breakthroughs that Unique Processes like Mary

Anne's provide. They're looking for the experience of being given direction where they are confused, confidence where they feel isolated, and capability where they feel powerless.

Transforming a Unique Process into an "experience monopoly."
It is obvious from looking at Mary Anne Ehlert's progress that she has created a great deal of success, satisfaction, and significance for herself in ways that would have been impossible by simply selling financial products. With regard to the four essential freedoms that we discussed at the beginning of this section — time, money, relationship, and purpose — Mary Anne has made extraordinary gains in both her professional and personal life. This has occurred after only a few years of being in the marketplace with her process. Much more progress and achievement lie ahead. From my vantage point of being a coach to many Unique Process Advisors, I see Mary Anne heading toward what I call an "experience monopoly." This is a permanent competitive advantage in the financial services marketplace that is only possible, I believe, for entrepreneurial advisors with Unique Processes. Based on the experiences of more than a hundred advisors, I have identified the key components of the monopoly, which, once it is established, can be protected with the legal tools of patents, copyrights, and trademarks:

- The Unique Ability and passion of a single entrepreneur is transformed into a problem-solving process.

- The process is directly focused on the unique dangers, opportunities, and strengths of a specific clientele.

- The process provides new forms of leadership, relationship, and creativity that are missing in the marketplace.

- The entrepreneur is able to expertly package this process and give the process a brand identity in the marketplace. Whenever somebody in the industry mentions his name, they immediately recognize his Unique Process.

- This private brand is under the exclusive creative control of the entrepreneur.

- The clientele undergo a transformative experience in relation to their most pressing concerns and issues. They feel a sense of personal direction, confidence, and capability that makes them optimistic about the future.

- The entrepreneur is compensated directly by the clientele for the unique value they receive — which they can't obtain anywhere else.

- The entrepreneur is able to use growing profits to build an organization around the process. This increases the reach and impact of the process in the marketplace.

- The growing success of the process and organization attracts talent, resources, and capital from other places in the industry, and from the general society and economy.

- All of the intellectual property being continually created within the process is systematically protected by patents, copyrights, and trademarks — so that it becomes impossible for any other organization to create or claim a similar consumer experience.

Outside of control. When I showed these "experience monopoly" components to Mary Anne Ehlert and other Unique Process Advisors, they all agreed that my analysis corresponded to their entrepreneurial experiences. Mary Anne is now considered the "go-to" authority in the United States for families with special needs. Her process and organization were recently featured in an ABC newscast. Within a matter of weeks, she and her team began receiving up to 50 inquiries a day from interested families. In addition, a recent announcement of new capabilities has been released to over three million Internet users, and is expected to generate hundreds of thousands of inquiries. The more progressive corporate and government institutions are now looking to her for guidance on how they can reform and transform their offerings to families. Hundreds of specialists in a wide range of professions have contacted her in order to become licensed to deliver The Process for Protected Tomorrows. All this is taking place for Mary Anne outside the control of financial corporations and regulatory agencies. As far as the corporation where she was originally licensed is concerned, its compliance lawyers still don't think what she is doing will work.

Models of freedom. Looking back to the four freedoms, Mary Anne and other Unique Process Advisors are enjoying them all — with much more to come. They are escaping from the bureaucratic controls and legal traps of the financial services industry. In doing so, they are creating new models for value creation that tens of thousands of advisors can follow. The Advisor Century, then, is for the advisors who create their own "experience monopolies."

3.

A Century Of Usefulness For Entrepreneurial Advisors

Part 3

The
Advisor
Century

Part 3:
A Century Of Usefulness
For Entrepreneurial Advisors

In 1931, an Austrian mathematician named Kurt Gödel made a breakthrough that explains why the microchip revolution is causing so much complexity and confusion in 21st-century life. It also explains why Unique Process Advisors are going to be some of the most useful people on the planet over the next hundred years. Gödel proved in his "incompleteness theorem" that we can never be inside of a system and fully understand the system that we are in.[11] In other words, if you are inside of a system — let's say an organization — you can't see what that organization looks like from the outside.

The longer you are in an organization and the more you have invested in your status within it, the less likely you are to understand what's going on outside of it.

When he read Gödel's paper, Albert Einstein predicted that this insight would be the most important new thought for the entire 20th century and beyond.

The Usefulness Economy. My own response to Gödel's theorem has been to formulate a concept that I call "The Usefulness Economy," which has the following principles.

1. Organizational blindness. The larger an organization is, the blinder its members, as a collective, become to outside changes.

2. Individual complexity. A single individual is far more complex than the biggest organization.

3. Endless desire. No matter how good something is, people will always eventually want something that's new, better, and different.

4. Infinite aspirations. The interests, needs, and aspirations of individuals are always expanding in unpredictable ways.

5. Constant differentiation. Every individual always wants to differentiate himself or herself, in some important way, from everyone else.

6. Timely usefulness. The single most important human value is always "usefulness in the moment."

7. Self-improving process. Growing usefulness always comes in the form of an evolving, self-improving process.

This concept of The Usefulness Economy helps explain why bureaucratic organizations in the financial services industry — and everywhere else in global society — are in a general state of turmoil, disintegration, and breakdown. It explains why consumers of every product, service, and experience in developed countries are increasingly dissatisfied with large organizations. It explains why so many individuals are actively looking for unique, alternative ways of satisfying their immediate and long-range needs and aspirations. And it explains why Unique Process Advisors have such a useful future ahead of them throughout the 21st century.

The usefulness principles. With this future in mind, I now want to go more deeply into each of the principles to show how Unique Process Advisors will become increasingly useful as bureaucracies fail. Each principle demonstrates why bureaucracies cannot deal with the demands and requirements of the microchip-driven world and why Unique Process Advisors are ideally positioned to create an entirely new kind of transformative marketplace.

Principle 1: Organizational blindness.
The larger an organization is, the more blind and deaf its members, as a

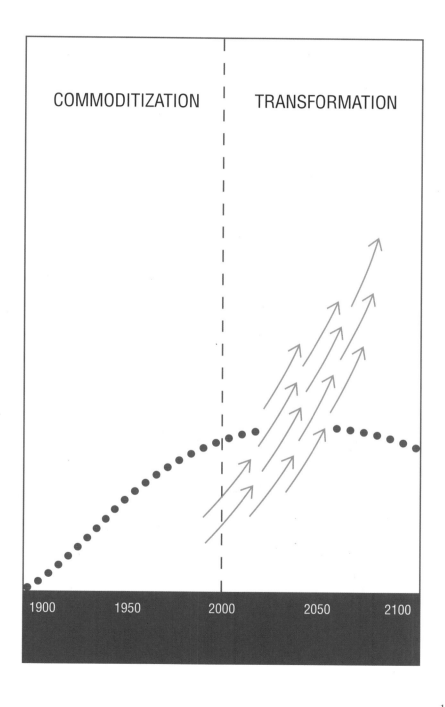

collective, become to outside changes. In the age of the microchip, many bureaucracies are becoming obstacles to human progress.

In the 19th and 20th centuries, large numbers of individuals saw their position within industrial societies determined by their relationship with large organizations. This is no longer the case. In the 21st century, individuals will be empowered by resources, capabilities, and opportunities that are being made available through the microchip revolution. The microchip revolution guarantees that the speed of unpredictable change in the marketplace will always be accelerating. This means that bureaucracies will continue to become worse at understanding and responding to changes in their marketplaces. Huge opportunity exists for entrepreneurs to be useful in ways that large organizations cannot be.

These opportunities to be useful will be greatest for those entrepreneurs who are financial advisors with Unique Processes.

Principle 2: Individual complexity.
A single individual is far more complex, intelligent, and adaptable than the biggest organization. When individuals are empowered with microchip-based tools, the complexity of their behavior increases, and bureaucracies cannot keep up.

Where the needs of individuals are predictable, bureaucracies will always have a use. But as long as people continually change their minds, their conditions, and their aspirations, something more responsive and adaptable is required.

Unique Process Advisors are in the best position to respond to the complex needs of individuals who have been empowered in unpredictable ways by microtechnology.

Principle 3: Endless desire.
No matter how good something is, people will always eventually want something that's new, better, and different.

Consumers in all industries now equate usefulness with constant innovation. This attitude greatly influences where people want to work, shop, and invest. Because entrepreneurial enterprises are capable of constant innovation, they always appear useful. As a result, young people today want entrepreneurial careers, not bureaucratic ones. Where price is not too great an issue, they often prefer to buy from entrepreneurial enterprises rather than large bureaucratic corporations. Increasingly, the smart money in the investment markets goes to promising and fast-growing entrepreneurial ventures, at the expense of bureaucratic organizations where all excitement and growth are in the past.

The most popular entrepreneurs in the 21st century will be Unique Process Advisors who provide evolving lifetime structures that allow people to satisfy their expanding needs and desires while bypassing bureaucratic limitations.

Principle 4: Infinite aspirations.

The interests, needs, and aspirations of individuals are always expanding in unpredictable ways. Bureaucratic conformity sees these aspirations as a threat, whereas for entrepreneurs seeking new ways to be useful, they offer a wealth of opportunity.

Microtechnology, especially now because of the Internet, gives individuals endless new ways to express their interests and utilize their skills. Each new interest brings with it new needs or aspirations that can be addressed by entrepreneurs. Each new evolution of the microchip, then, reinforces the strengths of entrepreneurs, and puts bureaucracies at a greater disadvantage.

Unique Process Advisors will be key players in helping millions of individuals to create custom-designed careers and lives that have expanding empowerment and opportunity.

Principle 5: Constant differentiation.

Every individual always wants to differentiate him or herself, in some important way, from everyone else. During the Industrial Age, people were content with equal membership in large collectives. Now that they are globally connected by microchip capabilities, individuals prefer to be "creatively unequal."

Many scholars studying this subject believe that the microchip not only undermined industrialization but also destroyed socialism. In the 19th century, socialists and communists predicted that industrial bureaucracies would lead to socialist utopias where everyone was equal. Of course, wherever these dreams were acted upon, they ended in disaster. That's why most people today resist the idea of socialist equality. Societies and economies built around the microchip offer people endless opportunities to differentiate themselves in the ways that they work, play, and live. Because people are increasingly connected by personalized technology, they no longer feel the need to be members of bureaucratic collectives. Industrial Age ideals of equality have given way to microchip-generated ideals of individuality and "creative inequality." This trend favors entrepreneurial diversity over bureaucratic conformity.

Unique Processes, by their very nature, enable individuals to plot out unique paths in every part of their lives. Unique Process Advisors will serve as key guides and supporters of "creative inequality."

Principle 6: Timely usefulness.
The single most important human value is always "usefulness in the moment." Bureaucratic organizations are slow to respond to consumer needs, and their structure makes it increasingly difficult to do so. Entrepreneurial enterprises are more responsive and can continually improve.

Stories about bureaucratic indifference and lack of service are the stuff of legend in every country. Bureaucracies do things on their schedule, ignoring everyone else's. They do things according to their priorities, not anyone else's. When consumers have no choice, they put up with this treatment. But when far better alternatives becomes available, they jump at them — and never look back. In every situation, people prefer choices that offer "usefulness in the moment" — value provided when and where it's most needed. The deeper the value provided at the right time, the more people appreciate it. When the value is continually timely and unique, people stay with it forever.

The basis of a Unique Process is The D.O.S. Conversation, which identifies people's most crucial issues and confirms their sense of urgency around addressing them. When a Unique Process Advisor implements solutions to address these issues quickly, clients feel enormous appreciation.

Principle 7: Self-improving process.

Growing usefulness always comes in the form of self-improving processes. Because they have the wrong kind of processes, bureaucracies seldom increase their usefulness over time. Only entrepreneurs have processes that can become continually more useful.

Bureaucracies are difficult to improve because individuals inside of them are not rewarded for telling the truth about what's working and what's not. Since most bureaucratic personnel are cut off from the outside, they don't get timely corrective feedback from the marketplace. And when it does come, they don't welcome it. Entrepreneurs, on the other hand, are in constant, direct, evolving relationships with their clientele. Feedback from clients and customers comes in the form of more money or no money. Lots of referrals or no referrals. New opportunities or no new opportunities. This is always very enlightening, and the learning is immediate. Entrepreneurs, therefore, are much more committed to self-improvement as an ongoing process because the rewards for telling the truth are much greater, and punishments for not doing so are more severe.

Unique Process Advisors have a great advantage over other entrepreneurs because their entire business is always based directly on the most important dangers, opportunities, and strengths of their clientele. Whenever these issues change, the process immediately improves to provide new and better solutions.

The microchip economy is rapidly transforming bureaucratic failures into "raw material" for entrepreneurial innovation and value.

If the principles of The Usefulness Economy provide an accurate assessment of the century ahead, then we are clearly at the threshold of something very new and different: *a world where bureaucracies will continually be replaced by networks of entrepreneurial Unique Processes.* I believe this is already beginning to occur in the financial services industry. Mary Anne Ehlert's Process for Protected Tomorrows shows why and how this takes place. The "why" is that bureaucratic organizations in different sectors are failing to provide individuals with the resources and support that they need. The "how" is a D.O.S.-based Unique Process that identifies all of the issues, integrates all of the resources, and creates entirely new capabilities to bring about superior solutions, both short-term and long-term.

What Mary Anne has done is utilize bureaucratic failures as an opportunity to create an entirely new kind of entrepreneurial enterprise.

One way I have found it useful to think about bureaucratic organizations, especially in the financial services industry, is to think about all of them as *raw material*. In other words, a great deal of what bureaucracies are and do can be transformed into more productive activities and outcomes. They are the best that a previous age could produce. Even now, many bureaucracies have talent, resources, and areas of focus that can be transformed into entrepreneurial initiatives and breakthroughs. So, when I use the term raw material, I mean the following:

- Bureaucracy was a form of organization that was very important and useful for a hundred years, but is now disintegrating because it's not responsive and self-improving in the face of changes caused by microtechnology.

- The build-up of bureaucratic organizations in the 20th century was massive, so there are enormous quantities of resources inside of them that can be better utilized in entrepreneurial endeavors.

- In every instance where bureaucracies are still in control, critical problems are being caused, and not being solved. These problems are all opportunities for entrepreneurial innovations.

- Every problem and deficiency in the world caused by the failure and disintegration of bureaucracy can be remedied by entrepreneurs with Unique Processes.

- The greatest opportunities for utilizing the "raw material" of bureaucratic failure will be captured by Unique Process Advisors who uniquely combine the capabilities of financial expertise with a deep grasp of human psychology.

The Bureaucratic Transformation. These five points make up a concept that I call "The Bureaucratic Transformation" — the complete utilization of everything bureaucratic in the world as a creative platform for innovating entrepreneurial alternatives. Since the amount of bureaucracy in the world is still extraordinary, the opportunities for entrepreneurism will be even greater. The Bureaucratic Transformation can be seen as the culmination of these other concepts that were introduced earlier in this book:

- **The Great Crossover:** Hundreds of millions of individuals will make the journey from economic childhood to economic adulthood during the 21st century. *They will do this, in large part, by eliminating their dependency on bureaucratic structures and processes in all sectors of the economy and society.*

- **The Microchip Revolution:** The introduction of microchip-based tools, systems, and processes into all areas of human activity. *For the most part, this revolution is continually generated by individual entrepreneurs and entrepreneurial enterprises with the aim of bypassing, undermining, and destroying inefficient bureaucracies in all sectors.*

- **The Commoditization Trap:** Being caught in a situation where the products and services that are the basis for one's livelihood are losing their profitability and value in the face of lower-priced competition. *One of the more important impacts of The Commodization Trap is that thousands of bureaucratic organizations and tens of millions of bureaucratic jobs are continually rendered obsolete or redundant.*

- **Economic Adulthood:** A condition of being increasingly in control of one's personal future, in all areas of life. *Individuals who work inside large bureaucracies, regardless of their status, face the opposite situation.*

- **Microchip Friendly:** The ability to use microchip-based tools and systems to increase personal productivity, opportunity, and usefulness, without regard to organizational hierarchy. *This goes directly against the top-down, hierarchical culture of subordination, deference, and conformity that enables bureaucratic organizations to function.*

- **The New Wealth:** A state of individual existence in a global economy characterized by neverending growth in 12 areas of self-determination. This existence represents the cutting edge of what is possible in a 21st-century world governed by microtechnology. *Very little of this "growth wealth" is possible for those who work for bureaucratic organizations — except for a few top executives, and then only for short periods of time.*

- **The Transformative Agenda:** A set of positive conditions necessary for individuals to make continual progress in the global economy. *Virtually all of these conditions are unavailable to most individuals who are bureaucratic employees.*

- **The Crossover Concerns:** A set of emotional and psychological anxieties that is associated with the crossover to economic adulthood. *Being dependent on bureaucratic organizations makes each of these anxieties more persistent and permanent.*

- **Complexity Consciousness:** Wisdom about how microtechnology is making life continually more complex for everyone, with an understanding of how to transform this global condition into endless entrepreneurial opportunities. *Working life inside of bureaucracies becomes more complicated and conflicted in response to increased complexity; things never simplify, with the result that the opportunities for personal progress and satisfaction are continually shrinking.*

- **Ceiling of Complexity:** A measurement of the limit of an individual's ability to deal effectively with complexity in the world. The higher a person's ceiling, the more successful he or she is at taking advantage of changes. For some individuals, the Ceiling of Complexity can be continually raised. For other people, it cannot. *Individuals often seek employment in bureaucratic organizations because they have a low Ceiling of Complexity. They hope that the organization will shield them from changes in the outside world. In some cases this still works. In most cases in the future, it won't.*

- **The Four Freedoms:** Four ways of being free — time, money, relationship, and purpose — that are increasingly possible for people who have chosen an entrepreneurial way of making a living, and are successful at it. *These freedoms are not available to bureaucratic employees, regardless of how high up they are in an organization.*

- **The D.O.S. Conversation:** A means of identifying, through open-ended, future-focused discussion, an individual consumer's most crucial dangers, opportunities, and strengths. This recognition serves as the basis for creating personalized value in a completely non-commoditized fashion. *This is something that bureaucratic individuals are not capable of doing, because there is no encouragement or reward for them to do so.*

- **Unique Process:** A structured approach to transforming the most important D.O.S. (dangers, opportunities, strengths) issues of a client or customer into a unique problem-solving system. The Unique Process serves as the foundation for a long-term relationship whose value to the clientele is independent of commoditized products and services. *All bureaucracies are focused on development and distribution of commoditized products, services, and experiences to mass markets and audiences. Developing unique relationships with people is neither desirable nor possible.*

- **Experience Monopoly:** The unique emotional value that clients experience as they proceed through the value creation stages of a Unique Process. This unique client experience can be transformed into intellectual property in the marketplace through patents, copyrights, and trademarks. *All of this is completely foreign to the commoditized experiences that bureaucracies produce. Bureaucratic work does not provide unique emotional value in the marketplace. Nor can bureaucratic workers claim innovations as their own intellectual property.*

The double opportunity. This is where we are now. The microchip revolution is giving us two freedoms: freedom from and freedom to. Freedom from bureaucracy, and freedom to be more entrepreneurial. The two freedoms feed off each other. As bureaucracies break down, people are forced to become more entrepreneurial. As entrepreneurism expands, bureaucracy becomes irrelevant and obsolete. The failure of bureaucracies creates opportunities for entrepreneurial alternatives. The success of entrepreneurial alternatives prompts the best and brightest bureaucrats to jump ship. They take everything with them that is still valuable: ideas, knowledge, capabilities, and capital. All of these increasingly move from the old to the new. Because this entire process is fueled by faster and smarter microchips, the bureaucracies get worse at a faster rate while new entrepreneurial ventures expand at a faster rate. This is how The Bureaucratic Transformation is taking place. It is one of the most interesting and significant crossovers in human history. It will all largely happen within the span of a single human lifetime. Nothing this big and important has ever happened so quickly, and most of us are lucky to be part of it.

This discussion brings us full circle back to The Usefulness Economy. There is a great need for a new kind of organizational structure. Bureaucracy rose in the world because of industrialization. Massive machinery required massive organizations. To keep the machinery profitable, people had to be trained to be machine-like. Entrepreneurism is on the rise because of the microchip. Now people need to be trained to be as creative and cooperative as possible. In the old system, they needed to show up and do what they were told. In the new system, they need to think and grow. They need to dream and achieve. A new kind of organizational structure is needed where people can be creative and cooperative for an entire lifetime, an organizational structure that continually supports their ability to think and grow, and continually evolves to encourage their dreams and achievements. This new kind of organization will be the most useful that has ever existed.

It already exists. Fortunately, this kind of organization already exists. It arises naturally around a Unique Process. Mary Anne Ehlert has one kind of Unique Process, which we've already described. Among our Strategic Coach clients, there are hundreds of others. They have been created in many different industries, but the majority of them are in financial services. The power of every Unique Process comes from three factors. First, entrepreneurs are the only ones who can create it. Second, the focus of a Unique Process is always on the dangers, opportunities, and strengths (D.O.S.) of specific clients or customers. Everything always begins and ends with D.O.S. Third, the Unique Process structure always improves as the clientele think and grow, dream and achieve, thus giving the organization a clear and natural growth path.

For these reasons, the Unique Process provides an answer to Professor Gödel's incompleteness theorem. Unlike bureaucrats who always get trapped inside of their own system, Unique Process Advisors are always able to get outside of theirs. In their attempt to be internally complete and consistent, bureaucracies cut themselves off from ideas, innovations, and talent. Unique Processes are always open to new, better, and different information from clients. Resources, capabilities, and opportunities flow to this better approach. *From the standpoint of their clientele, bureaucracies always become less useful, while Unique Processes become more useful.*

In the next three sections, we are going to show just how useful Unique Process Advisors can be. It's important to remember that we are only in the first decade of this new organizational form. We are still in the trial-and-error period. But we know it works. Even the early successes have been extraordinary. The advisors that we will spotlight in these next sections are all pioneers. Each of them was successful at selling commodities before creating their processes. Each of them has that rare combination of financial expertise and psychological wisdom. Each of them has a passion about creating a special kind of value, but in a completely different way. And each of them has become increasingly independent in an industry where many advisors are captive. It is this combination of independence, usefulness, and success that is now attracting many other financial advisors to these Unique Process pioneers. In examining their success, we will first focus on how they are transforming the lives and futures of their clientele. Then, we will examine how they are transforming the financial services industry. Finally, we will see how these Unique Processes are transforming society.

Usefulness 1:
Transforming Client Futures

Chuck Brewster, mentioned earlier in this book, has one of the simplest and most straightforward Unique Processes. It's called The 90 Day Check-Up System. Over his years as a financial advisor selling products, Chuck noticed that most of his clients had a poor grasp of their cash flow position. Based on hundreds of interviews, he identified 16 different factors that provided the best possible cash flow overview. When he provided this picture to his clientele, they were thrilled. Chuck noticed that they became much more confident about the present. They stopped beating themselves up about past mistakes. They became motivated to set more ambitious goals and start making short-term improvements in all areas of their finances. One client put it this way:

"This is the first time in my life that I feel I am in control."

Other clients had equally glowing comments:

"I've felt paralyzed about making all kinds of decisions. Now, I feel confident about moving forward."

Another individual confessed:

"I was afraid of knowing where I stood, because I've been sloppy with my money. Now, I feel that's all behind me. I'm better off than I thought."

Chuck's cash flow overview also encouraged clients to start talking talking about money with their families: *"I've always kept my wife in the dark about our finances because I didn't really know the score. It's caused a lot of tension and stress. Now, she's excited about what's happening. I understand it, and so does she."*

The software commitment. Chuck Brewster's 90 Day Check-Up System started off as a simple paper document, but he quickly transformed it into a software package. As he explains, "The software made it easier to use. The clients took me more seriously. The record-keeping and report-writing were a lot simpler — and it forced me to think it through more deeply."

But the biggest thing the software platform did was make it clear to Chuck that he had fundamentally transformed his advisory business. He noticed that he was presenting himself differently, and his clients were responding to him differently:

"Before, it was always this long drawn-out dance. I was trying to get a prospect or client around to buy a product, which was the only way I could get paid. I didn't want to spend too much up-front time with the individual. I didn't really want to know any more about their situation than what was needed to make a product presentation. I made a good living, but this always bothered me.

I honestly tried to be interested in them, but what I was really interested in was the commission. I think they always sensed this. Looking back, some of the situations make me cringe."

Over the last 30 years, I've noticed this same ethical ambivalence in many highly successful advisors who depend entirely on product sales for their income. They want to treat their clients as unique individuals, but when it comes down to the crunch, they're just the next sale. Then it's on to the next one, without looking back. When advisors only get paid for selling products — and only after the sale is official — they can't treat each person in a unique fashion. They can't continually cultivate and deepen the relationships over a long period of time. The time and money simply aren't there to do that. They are encouraged by the industry to make the relationships superficial and short, regardless of how much they might like them to be otherwise. The compensation system based on products only rewards quantity, not quality. Because they are paid only for selling commodities, they have to treat their clientele like commodities. In the process, they feel superficial, cheap, and unprofessional. They feel that they, too, are just a commodity.

Rewarded for relationship. Now, operating from within his Unique Process, Chuck finds that he loves spending more time with his clients. He learns everything he can about their problems and aspirations. The reason? Well, there are quite a few.

- **Paid up front:** Because he now gets paid up front for these discussions, Chuck has the security and confidence to go deep with his client discussions. He's already been paid for his time. He's been paid for his interest and his undivided attention. And he's been paid for his commitment to hearing all the issues — not just the ones that will lead to a product sale.

- **Lifetime capability:** The 90 Day Check-Up System provides an extraordinary capability to Chuck's clients — and they get it right up front. The first time they go through it, they know that this is something they can use for the rest of their life. They also know it's the best way of looking at their finances that they've ever had.

- **Client commitment:** Unlike in product sales, where clients never pay anything until the end, all of Chuck's clients are financially committed from the start. But their commitment is about far more than just money. Because they know they are building a lifetime capability for themselves, they are totally forthcoming with their issues and information. Because they know The 90 Day Check-Up System is going to help them, they make sure that Chuck knows everything that's crucial to moving forward.

- **Constant reinforcement:** When clients sign up for Chuck's system, they agree to come to his office every quarter for a scheduled two-hour meeting. Each time they come, Chuck reviews all 16 factors. They look at what's changed, where progress has been made, what the most crucial issues are for the next 90 days, what decisions have to be made, and what the most important actions are moving forward. By going through this analysis, his clients keep taking 90-day jumps. Every three months, things get clearer and better. Every three months, they become more confident and motivated.

- **Up-to-date gameplan:** The software package Chuck has designed documents each of the quarterly check-ups and prints out a new game-plan for the next 90 days. He reports that the clients love these three-page documents, which they keep in tabbed binders provided at the first meeting. He says, *"During the quarter, they keep pulling them out and looking over their progress and next steps. One of my clients told me that he now looks at his finances more each month than he used to do in ten years."*

- **Long-range thinking:** Because his clients are so confident about their present, they feel more confident about looking at their future. Goals that previously seemed impossible now look reasonable. Where before, some individuals lived month to month, they now start visualizing years and even decades ahead. Chuck says that he can see their minds growing. After each quarter's check-up, their futures get bigger.

- **Crucial partnership:** Chuck reports that his clients see him as crucial to their future success, satisfaction, and significance. He says, *"A lot of them see me as their most important advisor. They see their accountant maybe once a year, their lawyer less than that. Their banker doesn't know who they are, and their doctor never gives them more than 15 minutes. Their pastor or rabbi doesn't know anything about money and can't talk to them about their dreams.*

  They get to talk to me about everything that's going to make their lives better — and it happens, on schedule, every 90 days."

- **Constant referrals:** The word is spreading about what Chuck is doing. His clients continually introduce him to other people who need The 90 Day Check-Up System as badly as they did. They continually brag about their results, and attribute their progress to their relationship with Chuck. He says, *"When I was just selling product, I used to have to ask for referrals. It was like pulling teeth. Now the phone is always ringing."* And, as Chuck remarks, virtually every referral becomes a client: *"Unless I don't want them."*

- **Big product sales:** The irony is that Chuck is selling far more product inside of his Unique Process than he ever did when product was the only thing he had to sell: *"Sell is the wrong word. There's such a trust level inside of the process that the clients just tell me to handle things. The products are just part of the plan."* As a result, Chuck's commissions are now four times what they were before he created The 90 Day Check-Up System.

- **Ownership:** The confidence of his clients has gone up dramatically. But so has Chuck's:

"I think the biggest reason is that everybody loves what I've created, and I own it."

The 90 Day Check-Up System is Chuck Brewster's intellectual property. All the money he makes from it is his money. He doesn't ask any bureaucrat or regulator for permission. No one else can use it unless they pay him a licensing fee — and hundreds of other advisors are doing just that. This sense of ownership gives him a lot of confidence. But it also gives him pride: *"I know I am transforming the life of every client who enters the process for the better. Their lives were filled with confusion and doubt before they started. A lot of them didn't know what to do next — and now they're planning for things they couldn't have imagined. Their lives keep getting better. And I'm the one who gave them the tool."*

Every Unique Process transforms people's futures by turning complexity into simplicity.

Earlier in the book I defined *transformation* as raising someone's Ceiling of Complexity. Whenever you take the complexity in someone's life and make it simple for them, you've raised their ceiling, and you've transformed them. You've transformed their present, probably their past, and certainly their future. That's what Unique Process Advisors like Chuck Brewster do for their clients. This section of the book is on usefulness. The most useful thing you can do for another human being in the 21st century is continually help them to raise their Ceiling of Complexity. When you do this, you develop a lifetime relationship with them based on transformation.[12]

The Upward Spiral. It's not only the clients who get transformed. In The Strategic Coach Program, I talk to hundreds of Unique Process Advisors every quarter. They always say the same kind of things that Chuck Brewster says:

- Every time they help raise someone else's Ceiling of Complexity, they raise their own.

- Every time they they help someone else's future get bigger, their own future gets bigger.

- Every time their Unique Process helps someone get better, the Unique Process itself gets better.

- Every time they are useful with just one client, they become more useful with all of their clients.

All wound up. I call all of these advisor experiences, "The Upward Spiral." I call it this for two reasons: One, because the feelings of personal clarity, confidence, and capability keep getting better. Two, because the experience keeps feeding on itself. *You always feel you're rising to a higher level — and you* *know this will reliably keep happening.* You just have to stay inside of your Unique Process and keep improving it. From working with financial advisors since 1974, I know The Upward Spiral only happens in a predictable fashion with entrepreneurial advisors who have created Unique Processes. I've known many advisors who only sell products. I know many of them today. The product-only advisors who are in The Strategic Coach Program are great people — but they don't experience The Upward Spiral. From time to time, they'll have a client or two where this happens. But most of their clients are just a one-time sale. When it does happen, they don't know how to reproduce it. For the Unique Process Advisors, The Upward Spiral happens so frequently and predictably, they come to expect it. *It's normal* — the everyday experience of operating from within a Unique Process. Normal or not, predictable or not, it's still a rush. It's so energizing and motivating that advisors sometimes have trouble sleeping. One advisor reported, "I get so wound up, I can't wind down."

What I'm describing is a profound intellectual, psychological, and emotional experience that comes from knowing you're one of the most useful people on the planet.

Another example of this usefulness is provided by David Bach, who has become well known for his books, *Smart Women Finish Rich, Smart Couples Finish Rich,* and *The Automatic Millionaire.* The latter book, which achieved number one bestseller status in the five top book charts, came from two insights that David had during his 20 years as an advisor: One, that the big financial corporations were focused on people who were already millionaires, and were largely ignoring everyone else. Two, that there was no common-sense education in the marketplace about how to become a net millionaire. He observed that many people had the means to become wealthy, but lacked a strategy and a plan. His recent bestselling book, *The Automatic Millionaire Homeowner*, is now helping millions of individuals achieve home ownership, which becomes their vehicle for wealth creation. David has gone beyond his books to create in-person and Internet-based coaching programs that enable thousands of financial advisors to use The Automatic Millionaire[††] as a platform for helping their clientele.

From passion to process. Scott Keffer's passion is charitable giving. What he noticed as a financial advisor was that most charitable organizations need deeper relationships with their key donors and they need to attract many more potential donors. He recognized that motivating donors requires focusing on their D.O.S., not necessarily the D.O.S. of the organizations. There are tens of thousands of wealthy individuals who have the capacity to make significant contributions, but they don't understand how charitable giving can help them meet their own needs and yet still leave a legacy. At the same time, he noticed that the financial advisors who shared his passion were striking out in their attempts to work with charitable organizations and their donors.

Scott realized that he was dealing with three kinds of ignorance and inability, which needed an integrated solution. His Unique Process, The Donor Motivation Program**, brings all three parties together. Charities, wealthy individuals, and financial advisors become long-term partners. As a result, billions of charitable dollars are now being strategically targeted where they can do the most good.

The first objective of every Unique Process Advisor is to help his or her own clientele. But often, as these advisors realize what a breakthrough they have created for themselves, they put their wisdom and strategies into a form that can be used by other financial advisors. Mary Anne Ehlert, David Bach, and Scott Keffer have all embraced this approach. Again, this is part of the The Upward Spiral mentality. As Scott puts it, *"America is in a unique position. There are issues and opportunities. There's enough money, ingenuity, and heart to make a difference, that it's crazy to think in selfish, self-protective terms. The biggest problem isn't scarcity of resources, but scarcity of teamwork. What I've created helps bridge the giving gap that exists between wealthy individuals, advisors, and charities, and brings extraordinary teamwork into the whole area of charitable giving. The more players we can get involved, the better the future will be for everyone."*

Bigger pies, more processes. Essentially, all Unique Process Advisors believe that the economic pie keeps getting bigger. They also believe that there are many different kinds of pies being created by the microchip revolution. Another financial advisor who subscribes to the bigger pie philosophy is Dan Taylor, who has created and is implementing several Unique Processes. The one that he sees as most crucial for millions of individuals is The Parent Care Solution. This process was developed out of Dan's own experience dealing with his father, who developed Alzheimer's disease. Dan discovered that this ordeal was shared by adult children across the U.S. who are responsible for caring for their aging parents:

"The baby boom generation is going to spend decades handling this emotional, psychological, and financial burden. In some cases, it's going to last 30 years — and hardly anyone is prepared for this responsibility."

Dan developed The Parent Care Solution around six in-depth conversations that adult children need to have with their parents. These conversations cover finances, housing, medical care, assistance, estate planning, and legacies. His own clients have been extremely relieved by the results of these conversations. One of them told Dan:

"You don't realize what a burden this is until you actually have the ability to deal with it. What I discovered was that it was a huge problem for my parents as well. We were both worried about it but there wasn't an easy way to talk about it. As soon as we started inside of this structure, we were amazed how quickly everything happened. It was six months of organized cooperation, instead of 20 years of growing tension and then a big mess at the end."

Remarkably bigger futures. Dan Taylor's process provides *freedom from* and *freedom to* for both the adult children and their parents. Both parties are freed up from anxiety, indecision, paralysis, foreboding, and resentment. Both are freed up to enjoy their mutual relationship, knowing that everything is planned for and handled. The Parent Care Solution maximizes the commitment, resources, and goodwill of families to achieve the best possible quality of life for everyone involved.

Remarkably useful. Dan Taylor immediately recognized that his intellectual property provided a marketplace opportunity for thousands of financial advisors. He has developed this into an educational and licensing program that hundreds of professionals — including accountants and lawyers — are using to support their clientele across America. One of the first advisors to implement Dan's process reported back, "This is the first time that I feel confident in bringing up these issues with my clients. Before, they always had the suspicion that I was trying to sell them another policy. Which, of course I was. I didn't have anything to offer them. Now, instead of being an annoyance, I am the main problem-solver. And, yes, I'm getting well paid for helping them solve the biggest problem in their lives right now."

Another advisor said, "I feel right now that I am the most useful person that these people know. Leading them through these conversations is also the most satisfying thing I've done in my career. When everything's finished, the money will be my smallest reward. It used to be the only reward."

Why Unique Processes are extraordinarily useful in ways that commoditized products can never be.

The Unique Process represents an entirely new way for financial advisors to operate in the marketplace. It's not just an incrementally better way of operating, it's an exponentially superior way of creating relationships, designing solutions, and achieving results.

Put simply, there is no comparison between being a product-based advisor and a Unique Process Advisor. The Unique Process is advantageous in every way.

The Process Advantage. Because I have witnessed more than ten years of results from hundreds of Unique Process Advisors, I feel confident in describing the following advantages that having a Unique Process gives to advisors:

1. Psychological integrity. One of the most important thing that happens from working within a Unique Process is that advisors become better human beings. By this, I mean that they feel better about themselves, both as professionals and as people. They no longer suffer from the ethical strains that come from recommending product-based solutions just to get a commission.

2. Transformative conversations. Technology has negative as well as positive impacts. One of the biggest negatives is a the commoditization of communication — especially in the business world. Every Unique Process is based on a D.O.S. Conversation that focuses on the client's most important sources of fear, excitement, and confidence. Allowing these issues to come to the surface has a transformative impact on both the client and the advisor. All D.O.S. Conversations identify the central goals, ideals, and values that motivate both the client and the advisor.

3. Referral universes. Every financial advisor wants to have good referral networks. The Unique Process creates referral universes. The desire to refer among Unique Process clientele is virtually unlimited because the experience is so ethical and transformative and the results are so extraordinary and lasting.

4. Products just tools. Instead of being the main vehicle for an advisor's success, financial products are now simply tools for implementing strategies and solutions. By reducing products to the status of tools, the Unique Process enables advisors to reduce financial bureaucracies to the simple status of tool-makers.

5. Competitors become customers. A Unique Process does more than just enable an advisor to bypass all competition: It transforms competitors into customers. All the Unique Process Advisors cited as examples in this book have now created programs by which other advisors can license the use of their intellectual property. This teamwork around a Unique Process evolves into expanding networks of cooperative partnerships.

6. Cash flow predictability. Product-based advisors start each year more or less from square one. No matter how good their last year was, they face sales uncertainty in the coming one. Some try to hedge this problem by getting paid for their assets under management, but this has the long-range effect of making them passive and commoditized. It becomes harder to demonstrate how they are creating new value for their clientele. It also becomes harder to justify why companies should continue paying them the same fees. Over time, the clients change their minds, and so do the companies. A Unique Process invariably establishes a long-term relationship in which new opportunities for value creation continually emerge as The D.O.S. Conversation becomes deeper. As more and more clients enthusiastically pay larger upfront fees, advisors experience growing cash flow predictability, which enables them to plan for and invest in a bigger future.

7. Freedom from bureaucracy. The previous six advantages contribute to a growing freedom from having to deal with bureaucracies and bureaucratic personnel. The progressive impact of creating and utilizing a Unique Process provides immense psychological freedom. There is no need to depend upon a large organization for direction, confidence, or capability. Because Unique Process Advisors are paid directly by their clients, their dependency on commissions and fees also decreases significantly, providing financial freedom.

Free yourself, free others. The Unique Process Advisors we are describing have freed themselves from dependency on financial bureaucracies. In the next section, we are going to show how their Unique Processes provide the means for thousands of other advisors to become free. As this occurs, the entire financial services industry will be transformed in extraordinary ways.

Usefulness 2:
Transforming The Industry

Doug Andrew started off as a life insurance agent in the 1970s, but is now the creator of a Unique Process network that involves thousands of entrepreneurs from five different industries. In the course of D.O.S. Conversations with his insurance prospects and clients, Doug identified a hidden source of wealth very few individuals realized they possessed. He noticed that the equity in their homes was essentially "trapped capital." In other words, it wasn't doing any work for them except showing up on the positive side of their balance sheet. It was passive rather than dynamic wealth. Over the years, the value of their homes would appreciate, but this increase in wealth was minor compared with what could happen if it was redeployed inside of an insurance policy.

Doug told them that by keeping their capital trapped inside of their homes, they were literally "missing a fortune."

But they could correct this problem very quickly. By using a home equity loan, they created a second wealth creation vehicle — using the same capital. They still retained ownership of their homes, but now they also owned a valuable insurance policy, which had both a death benefit and a growing cash value. This second vehicle was also creditor-proof.

Much bigger game. Doug transformed his "missed fortune" discovery and innovation into a Unique Process called The True Wealth Transformer[††], which he first made available to his own clients. This new approach transformed the future possibilities of his clientele overnight — as well as doing the same for his insurance practice. But Doug realized immediately that this was a much bigger game than his own practice. When he told other life insurance agents about his approach, many of them wanted to learn it. This led to the creation of a school where hundreds of life insurance professionals have transformed their careers and their futures by acquiring an entirely new framework for creating value for their clientele. But since Doug's solution involved real estate, a steady stream of mortgage lenders and real estate agents asked if they could join his program. Within a matter of four years, his network of licensed practioners exceeded 2,000 individuals. Then groups of accountants and lawyers asked to participate. Literally, tens of thousands of homeowners were now doubling the dynamic value of their capital through The True Wealth Transformer. It was at this point that Doug Andrew realized he was an Industry Transformer™.

"One morning I woke up thinking, 'What have I done? I was just trying to improve my own business; now look what's happened. This could affect millions of people. This could totally transform the usefulness of home ownership. It totally expands the usefulness of life insurance. It works for everybody. Everybody involved wins.'"

Extraordinary future. By combining three financial tools — home equity, a loan, and an insurance policy — into a single Unique Process, he was multiplying the wealth of consumers, and the incomes of five different kinds of professionals. When he began to think about the implications for each of these industries, and for the economy as a whole, his vision of the future was extraordinary.

The "Missed-Fortune" brand. It was a big future that several large corporations could also see. Doug was contacted by one of America's biggest publishers to create a series of books under the brand name, "Missed Fortune." The first book sold over 100,000 copies in the first year. This publishing success, of course, brought Doug thousands of interested advisors and tens of thousands of prospective clients. Because he and his team couldn't deal personally with these consumers, Doug created a service providing the advisors in his network with high-quality sales leads. Working with his publisher, he has expanded and deepened his wealth creation philosophy and methodology.

By leveraging his training school, his books, his network of licensed professionals, and the growing volume of reader inquiries, Doug and his team plan to create a wealth creation system for entrepreneurs and consumers in every postal code area in the U.S.

He says, *"I truly believe that we are going to multiply the wealth of Americans significantly. We're talking about hundreds of millions of people who are going to benefit from this. We're talking about trillions of dollars in transformed capital. The impact on the mortgage, real estate, and life insurance industries is also going to be transformative."*

In addition to publishing corporations, Doug has also been increasingly approached by insurance companies. They are now creating specialized policies, services, and other financial products to be used exclusively inside of his national Unique Process network. The senior executives in these companies can barely believe the opportunity that Doug Andrew has created for them. His Unique Process has taken a mature industry and given it an entirely new purpose and future.

Entrepreneurial advisors are transforming the financial industry in ways that are incomprehensible and impossible for bureaucrats.

I have had the opportunity to confer with Doug continually throughout this entire adventure. Every time he comes to his Strategic Coach workshop, I catch up on his progress and share with him the Unique Process innovations that other entrepreneurs are creating. In analyzing his and their successes, I have identified a concept that I call "The Entrepreneurial Bypass." It explains, I think, why only entrepreneurs like Doug Andrew can bring about the continual transformation of the financial services industry. Here are its key components:

1. Identify new value possibilities. Entrepreneurial advisors are the only ones who can and will conduct the kind of in-depth, comprehensive discussions with financial consumers that identify new forms of value creation.

2. Relationship-based R & D. Only individual advisors with long-term personal relationships can test out new value creation ideas in ways that are immediately beneficial for the client and profitable for the entrepreneur. This research and development of new concepts, processes, and methods can be done quickly and economically, with a very rapid learning curve. Because value is created from the very start, the research and development pays for itself and also deepens the relationship.

3. Maximum personal incentive. From the very start, Unique Process Advisors are motivated to succeed for four reasons. One, because the Process is their idea and they receive the full payoff. Two, because it's their capabilities and relationships that are in play — and they are immediately rewarded for improving both. Three, because they don't have to consult with anyone except their clients, and they don't have to get anyone else's agreement or permission to move forward. And, four, because the resulting innovation, if successful, enables them to differentiate themselves in ways that their competitors cannot quickly comprehend or copy.

4. No bureaucratic obstacles. The entire process of innovation and development takes place in the best possible conditions: Only entrepreneurs and consumers are involved — no bureaucrats. There is no political jealousy, resentment, or sabotage to worry about. There are no idea-killing policies or procedures to contend with.

5. Rapid evolution. In the hands of an active entrepreneur experimenting daily with clientele in the marketplace, an innovation evolves much more quickly than inside of a bureaucracy. The reason for this is that failures and mistakes mean something entirely different for entrepreneurs than for bureaucrats. For entrepreneurs, failure leads to learning and transformation. For bureaucrats, it can mean humiliation, demotion, and termination. *Entrepreneurial innovations can evolve through five improved versions faster than a bureaucratic innovator can evolve through one.*

6. Undetected bypasses. If a financial bureaucracy comes out with a new innovation, every other bureaucracy knows about it within 24 hours. If an entrepreneurial advisor is successful with an innovation, it may be years before the bureaucracies catch on to what's happening. Doug Andrew had already tested and proven his Unique Process and attracted hundreds of other advisors to his school and network before the first insurance companies realized the importance of what he had created. Bureaucrats are always the last players in any game where something new, better, and different is changing the world.

This Entrepreneurial Bypass explains why virtually all of the the most important client-based innovations in the 21st century will be created by Unique Process Advisors. These advisors will increasingly operate as Industry Transformers, continually bypassing everything that is depleted about their industry to create exciting new value. Recall our earlier discussion of Gödel's theorem. Gödel proved in his incompleteness theorem that we can never be inside of a system and fully understand the system that we are in. One implication of this theorem is "organizational blindness," the inability of people inside large organizations to grasp anything that exists outside of those organizations. Yet the same could be said for entire industries such as financial services.

For decades, advisors have operated inside of a highly complex system that people call the financial services industry. They've been trained to think of themselves first as brokers, insurance agents, and estate planners, and more recently as financial advisors, investment advisors, and financial planners — but not as entrepreneurs. When people ask what they do for a living, most are conditioned to respond with the specialized job title that appears on their business cards.

The danger, however, of adopting this career-identification is that it prevents them from grasping the extraordinary opportunities that exist outside of the conventional experience of the industry. Essentially, they are "trapped" within the industry. All of the industry's problems become their problems. All of the industry's messes become their messes. And the more consumed they are by the industry's baggage, the less value they can create for clients.

In The Advisor Century, however, a growing network of Industry Transformers will emerge. These are Unique Process Advisors who have the tools and capabilities to transform the way value is created in their industry.

Extraordinary ambition. What unites these Industry Transformers is an elevated conception of what it means to be a financial advisor in the 21st century. For many years, large financial services organizations have defined the parameters of this profession. They've decided who financial advisors are and what they should or should not be doing. Industry Transformers reject this cookie-cutter mentality. They are continually reshaping the profession by finding new, more exciting roles for financial advisors.

Consider Dan Taylor and his Parent Care Solution, which we profiled earlier. Dan recognized that there are certain things financial advisors do extremely well. They have a real ability to carry on intimate conversations with clients about delicate, emotionally-charged issues. They can help clients understand the financial dimensions of these issues. And they can develop comprehensive plans that preempt some of the dangers clients are facing.

Thousands of financial advisors have these basic skills, but before Dan Taylor came around, few advisors ever thought about applying them in the area of parent-care. Dan has developed an entirely new role for financial advisors in the selection, management, and administering of an elderly person's long-term care. And he has developed comprehensive training programs that will allow hundreds of other advisors to use this Unique Process and become a Parent Care Specialist[†††]. Every advisor who goes through Dan's training programs represents yet another advisor who has escaped from their organizational captivity and escaped from their dependency on product sales. And that's how an entire industry is transformed, one advisor at a time.

Intellectual capital company. While Dan Taylor has experienced great success with The Parent Care Solution, he continues to develop new Unique Processes, and explore new ways of creating and packaging intellectual capital. That's because Dan isn't just a financial advisor. Rather, he's an entrepreneur with a particular specialty in financial services. He isn't running a financial services company. He's running an intellectual capital company, with financial services as one of his distribution channels.

These two changes in outlook represent what I call the "double shift." If you think about your career in these terms, chances are you'll be much more excited about your future. All of the Unique Process Advisors featured in this book are essentially running intellectual capital companies. Their entire business is focused on packaging ever increasing amounts of new intellectual capital. They are continually looking for new ways to get their Unique Process out in the marketplace — hosting training programs and seminars, giving speeches, writing books, and publishing manuals. They are continually developing innovative licensing arrangements that allow other advisors to implement this wisdom in their own businesses.

That's because they grasp a simple insight: The more people who "plug into" a particular system, the more valuable and indispensable that system becomes. Nothing is more exciting than having thousands of industry professionals clamoring to get hold of your intellectual capital, and ready to pay significant licensing fees for the right to utilize the wisdom that you created and own.

Magnifying capabilities. When Unique Process Advisors leverage the entrepreneurial bypass and develop an intellectual capital company, they have enormous impact on the capabilities of everyone around them. The early 19th-century French economist Jean-Baptiste Say was one of the first people to employ the term "entrepreneur." He defined entrepreneurs as people who take resources from a lower level of productivity to a higher level of productivity.[13] That's what Unique Process Advisors do: They take the resources of an entire industry from a lower to a higher level of productivity.

The Unique Process Advisors we have profiled all have different passions and capabilities, but they are all introducing transformative solutions into situations where human ambitions, resources, and capabilities have been underutilized — or trapped by bureaucracy. In dozens of different marketplace areas, they are already helping millions of people raise their Ceiling of Complexity, achieve The New Wealth, and make the transition from economic childhood to economic adulthood. But for the entire financial industry to be transformed, something more must happen.

Financial bureaucrats, to survive and succeed, need to recognize their fundamental weakness so that they can take advantage of entrepreneurial innovation.

In 1997, I was a speaker at a conference of financial advisors. I ended up sitting next to a very successful sales manager for a large company. He said that he was ambivalent about the coaching I was providing to advisors, including some of his. On the one hand, he liked the improved results they were getting. On the other, he was was worried about how independent they were acting. I asked him why this was a problem. "Because," he said, "It's going to shorten my career." "Nonsense," I said. "Someone who has great skills and a great track record as a sales manager will always have great opportunities."

"Yes," he responded, "But I'm going to have to start hustling again. I'm really comfortable. I don't know if I want to work that hard again."

Past bigger than their future. This sales manager's remarks, while refreshingly honest, are the perfect expression of what I call a "status mentality": People look at the world this way when their past has become bigger than their future. Throughout the bureaucratic structures of the financial services industry, there are thousands of individuals who have a status mentality. They are living off the momentum of their previous efforts, achievements, and results. In some cases, they got to a high position simply by surviving, not by achieving. They have big titles, but it's not clear that they deserve them. They have big reputations, but not for anything they're doing today. They have big salaries and perks, but not for any contributions they are still making. They have power and control over the activities of others, but they are not producing anything new, better, or different. These individuals have status, but they don't have any useful ideas. Their concept of the industry is out of date.

Depletion of value. The phenomenon I have just described is true of virtually any industry in the world. It reflects the fact that, among any group of people, there are two career paths: One is toward continual self-improvement and value creation for others. The other is toward increased personal status and security. In the entrepreneurial world, the self-improvers dominate. In the bureaucratic universe, the status-seekers invariably win out. The reason, of course, goes back to our concept of The Usefulness Economy: Bureaucratic organizations become increasingly blind to their consumers.

There is a tipping point in every bureaucratic organization when it switches from being a value creator to being a value extractor. Instead of giving to their consumers, they begin taking from them. The resources of the organization are redirected to use by the senior executives and managers in the form of salaries, options, bonuses, benefits, pensions, and a wide variety of "daily comforts and conveniences." The focus of executive activity is achieving ever increasing status — at the expense of the organization's usefulness in the marketplace. As this situation worsens, the organization becomes depleted of the value that made it successful and important in the first place. The rot in organizations, like fish, begins in the head.

Breeding grounds for complacency. There are historical reasons why this value depletion has tended to be worse in financial services organizations. The biggest reason is that, in the United States, the various specialties — insurance, banking, investments, trusts — were kept separate from one another by legislation. It is only in the last two decades that competition has crossed the boundaries of these different sectors. For most of the 20th century, many of the corporations in financial services operated in a virtually competition-free environment. Internally, many of them were run like socialist utopias. Externally, they were managed like quasi-public utilities. This experience did not put an emphasis on capability, achievement, and innovation. Financial services at the corporate level proved an excellent breeding ground for complacency, incompetence, and self-satisfied stasis.

Who's the customer? The second reason why value depletion took hold is that most financial executives never understood that financial advisors were their real customers, In the life insurance industry, especially, there has always been this myth that the corporations had a direct relationship with consumers in the marketplace. This may be contractually true, but it has never been true from the perspective of an actual cooperative, creative relationship. Therein lies the biggest danger that financial bureaucracies face, initially, from the emergence of Unique Process Advisors. I highlight the word "initially" here because in the long run, Unique Process Advisors will be the permanent salvation of financial corporations. Not all corporations, of course, but certainly the best of them. Before explaining how this will happen, I'd like to explore more deeply this looming danger for financial bureaucracies, which I call "The Relationship Weakness." Here are its main aspects:

- **Systems people:** Corporate people are systems people. In the 21st century, most of the people who get to the top of financial bureaucracies were educated and trained to get there. Their business school education was systems-focused, not people-focused. Business success was described as a mastery of systems, not a mastery of human relationships.

- **Life by the numbers:** The same business education that gets bureaucrats to the top focuses on quantity, not quality. If it can't be measured and counted, it doesn't matter. The most admired people are the ones who are masters of the numbers. In corporate bureaucracies, people who know the numbers control the activities and futures of those who don't.

- **Internal ambitions:** A mastery of systems and numbers leaves many bureaucrats with an attitude that relationships are disposable. They are a tool for advancement. Being friendly is a strategy for promotion rather than a commitment to friendship.

- **Trapped by structure:** Once an individual sets out on the road to bureaucratic advancement, it is a lifetime commitment. Everything that happens inside of the corporate structure takes on political importance. A wrong move, at any time, can have serious consequences. Saying no is usually more advantageous than saying yes. Bringing someone else down is a good way to take oneself up. What happens outside is always of lesser daily importance than what is happening inside.

- **Reality-challenged:** Twenty years in bureaucracy is the usual time span for someone to reach a position of important leadership. There can be big payoffs if you have the aptitude and the right attitudes. But there's a price to be paid for this apprenticeship. The individual becomes more disconnected from the non-bureaucratic world — namely, where most human beings experience and live their lives. The real world of dangers, opportunities, and strengths — of open-ended conversations, possibilities, and futures — becomes a foreign place for those climbing the bureaucratic ladder. It's not that bureaucrats don't have real experiences and aspirations. It's just that they've had to specialize for so long in such a narrow pursuit for such a scarce prize, they've lost the ability to communicate and relate in many normal ways. The reality of non-bureaucratic existence is hard for them to grasp and respond to. They're not bad people, they're just disconnected in significant ways. They're increasingly disconnected from the lives and issues of clients and customers who purchase their products. As the microchip revolution speeds up, the disconnect between bureaucrats and consumers will widen.

The evolution of bureaucracy.

Depletion creates fertile ground for transformation, and the direction of this evolution for the financial services industry is already beginning to show. In the introduction to this book, I predict that the financial services industry will divide into two realms.

1. Super-corporations. One financial realm will be super-corporate in the form of global commoditizers. These most likely will be huge international banks that own dozens of insurance companies, mutual funds, and investment firms — as well as other specialized financial enterprises. They will operate across national borders and employ hundreds of thousands of workers. The economies of scale will be extraordinary, and the revenues of the largest firms will exceed the gross domestic products of many nation-states. The reason for their success will come from the ability to commoditize products and services on a global basis. These commodities will be distributed in a variety of ways: through their own captive organizations, through the Internet — and through vast networks of entrepreneurial advisors.

Where bureaucracy still makes sense. It is only at this level of super-organization that bureaucracy will make sense in the 21st century. Only through the continual consolidation of many smaller organizations into larger ones can bureaucratic structures and strategies be profitable. This has already been happening for 20 years. Where there were thousands of financial corporations, there are now hundreds. In the near future, the hundreds will become dozens. Millions of bureaucratic jobs and careers will continue to be eliminated as a powerful few global firms become larger. Many bureaucratic individuals will be forced, or will choose, to move over to the entrepreneurial side of the industry.

2. Super-entrepreneurs. The other realm will consist of super-entrepreneurs — in the form of thousands of Unique Process Advisors and their networks. Virtually all the client-focused creativity in the financial industry will come from these Unique Processes. The reason for this lies in the power of D.O.S. Conversations. Bureaucrats operating at the top of the super-corporations will have no contact with end-users in the marketplace. *Unique Process Advisors, on the other hand, will have extraordinary "deep support" relationships with these clients and customers.*

Economies of impact. It will be the Unique Process Advisors who identify the emerging needs of individuals in a world of unpredictable change. It will be the Unique Process Advisors who innovate the new forms of service and support that enable millions of individuals to gain greater direction, confidence, and capability in their lives and businesses. And it will be the Unique Process Advisors who transform their innovations into educational systems that enable thousands of other advisors to master these new forms of value creation. In addition, dozens of Unique Process Advisors will unite to create enormous "economies of impact." This will happen by linking up their innovations into "plug-and-play partnerships" where several processes can be applied simultaneously to provide comprehensive D.O.S. breakthroughs for individuals and organizations.

The smart bureaucracies will feed off the innovations of the smart entrepreneurs — and the entrepreneurs, in turn, will utilize the commodities produced by the bureaucrats.

Symbiotic relationship. What I am describing here is a symbiotic relationship between the best of the bureaucrats and the best of the entrepreneurs. It is also a relationship between what bureaucrats do best and what entrepreneurs do best. This relationship will succeed and grow because it makes sense for both parties. On the one hand, super-corporations can only succeed if they have access to new innovations and distribution channels. They are incapable of creating these on their own. They do not understand what is happening in the lives of individual clients and customers. The economic constraints of their organizations do not allow them to focus on individuals. All the inspiration for new commodities, therefore, will come from entrepreneurs. All the new need for commodities will be uncovered by entrepreneurs, and all the ways to use commodities will be pioneered by entrepreneurs.

Entrepreneurs, for their part, can only implement the strategies of their Unique Processes if they have access to highly effective and low-cost commodities. This is true in all sectors of the economy. *The best doctors will always need commoditized drugs, the best mechanics always need commoditized parts, and the best Unique Process Advisors will always need commoditized financial products.* At the end of the day, every Unique Process requires some kind of financial product to transform the client's situation. In many cases, several products are required. A super-corporation will be far better than individual entrepreneurs at developing, testing, packaging, and distributing these commodities. As more Unique Processes are created, there will be more possibilities for new kinds of products. Likewise, the better and more varied the products become, the more possibilities there will be for individual financial advisors to create and implement their Unique Processes.

A still bigger game. In the previous section, we described how Unique Process Advisors transform the futures of their clientele. In this section, we described how Unique Process Advisors, individually and in partnership, are transforming the financial services industry. We also suggested that it will be in the best interests of the financial corporations to create partnerships with Unique Process Advisors. The combination of economies of scale provided by super-corporations and the economies of impact provided by super-entrepreneurs will create an even bigger possibility: whole societies where the majority of individuals are moving from economic childhood to economic adulthood.

Usefulness 3:
Transforming Society

Unique Processes are transforming the futures of individual clients. They are transforming the financial services industry. Now we will examine "the bigger game," the use of advisor-generated Unique Processes to transform society as a whole.

Our basic premise is that in The Advisor Century, financial advisors will unleash their enormous potential as "social entrepreneurs." Social entrepreneurship is no different from any other form of entrepreneurship. It simply means bringing our societal resources from a lower to a higher level of productivity — creating powerful solutions to important social problems. As social entrepreneurs, Unique Process Advisors will increasingly operate as change-agents. They will be important participants in public dialogues at the local, state, and national levels. They will serve as influential leaders in the community and outspoken advocates for important causes. And they will do all of this while continuing to create extraordinary value for their clients.

The social consequences of economic childhood. We have argued throughout this book that the time has come for millions of people need to make the transition from economic childhood to economic adulthood. So many of our social problems — poverty, crime, broken families — occur because people are unable to get themselves out of economic childhood. They possess none of the tools, knowledge, or habits to take control of their financial affairs and overcome their dependency on large organizations. Government welfare programs designed to serve these individuals often worsen the problem by making them even more dependent. If people are unable to experience any meaningful growth and self-development, society is denied the productive contributions that empowered economic adults can provide.

Financial advisors can make enormous social contributions by leading people to greater financial independence and providing solutions in areas where government bureaucracies and other large organizations have left voids. In The Advisor Century, vast social energy will originate from the private, marketplace sphere. This trend goes against the frequent assumption that because something of value is produced in the marketplace with a profit motivation, little enduring social benefit can come from it.

For example, Mary Anne Ehlert operates as a social entrepreneur by creating a powerful solution for individuals with disabilities and their families in areas where the government's own social services bureaucracy has proven inadequate. For decades, government agencies and a few select non-profits have had a monopoly on the educational, healthcare, and housing services offered to people with disabilities. Through her Process for Protected Tomorrows, Mary Anne demonstrates that entrepreneurial creativity can have a far more empowering impact on special-needs families than any government program.

Mary Anne once spoke at the Institute of Persons with Disabilities in New York. Her Unique Process received an enthusiastic response. Some audience members were confused, however, about why Mary Anne was charging a fee for her services. They had an unquestioned expectation that people with disabilities should be serviced for free by society.

Mary Anne responded this way: "Let me ask, has the government done it for you yet? Have the not-for-profits been able to do what you want them to do? No? Then why wouldn't you be willing to pay a fee to get help?" This ability to charge for her services allows Mary Anne to provide personalized solutions to clients. The financial transaction between Mary Anne and her clients signals to both sides that a strong commitment exists for going forward with the relationship in a positive way.

Doug Andrew makes a similar impact. Doug's wisdom and methods can significantly increase the net worth and quality of life for millions of individuals. In America, Doug emphasizes, home ownership represents a $19 trillion investment. Yet $10 trillion of that is home equity, which earns nothing for the home owner. By helping his clients free up this lazy capital, Doug frees up more money for innovation and investment, more money for philanthropy and charitable-giving.

As is the case with every Unique Process that has been developed inside The Strategic Coach, these innovative solutions succeed by bypassing obsolete, incompetent, and disintegrating bureaucratic structures. Mary Anne and Doug either make bureaucracies irrelevant — or create ways in which bureaucratic resources can become useful in ways that were never before possible.

Here's a third example. Lee Brower was a very successful life insurance agent who specialized in the estate planning needs of wealthy families. His clients were typically the children or grandchildren of highly successful entrepreneurs who had created fortunes. Lee noticed after working for several years in this market that the normal approach to estate planning used by accountants, lawyers, and insurance agents tended to tear families apart. The way that money was handled and thought about in the planning process made enemies out of parents and children and pitted one child against another. This damage was on top of decades-old misunderstandings, conflicts, and resentments about money and possessions that had built up within many wealthy families.

In reviewing many of the D.O.S. Conversations he had conducted, Lee recognized a big opportunity. He identified a great desire on the part of these wealthy clients to transform their families' attitudes toward money in creative and constructive ways. As he got to the bottom of their issues, he discovered that the biggest motivations weren't about money at all. Their biggest desire was for integration. *What they really wanted was to have their families intellectually, psychologically, and emotionally united.*

Using his experience and insights from hundreds of conversations as raw material, Lee Brower created a Unique Process called The Quadrant Living Experience[†]. This process has many different dimensions, but its main impact is to transform wealthy families into positive forces for change in society. Instead of viewing the money as a problem, Lee helps wealthy families see it as the source of their biggest opportunities for achieving happiness, meaning, and significance. When he meets the head of a wealthy family for the first time, here is what he says:

"When you think about all of the money that your family has had over several generations — its impact on how you communicate and cooperate with one another — would you say that the money has had an empowering or disempowering impact?"

Lee reports that the answer is virtually always "disempowering." He remembers one man who became visibly upset with the question: *"It's torn us apart. Sometimes I wish we could get rid of all the damn money, so that we could all just appreciate each other again. It's made us hate each other."*

When he gets this kind of answer, Lee goes on:

"If I could show you a process that your whole family can go through, which uses your money to repair all of the damage and heal all of the injuries so that your family can be happy and whole, would you be interested in doing it?"

Precious opportunity. Lee gets far more yesses than noes. For many of these wealthy families, who can buy virtually anything they want, this is the most precious opportunity that has ever been offered to them. In spite of their wealth, family wholeness is the one thing they were never able to buy. In many cases, it's the choice between having all of their family's success and history be meaningless and painful versus meaningful and purposeful.

From burden to blessing. But Lee Brower's process goes far beyond just bringing a particular family back together. The Quadrant Living Experience works because it enables family members to see that they have the opportunity to be a transformative force for positive change in society. By going through Lee's process, the family members — as a unified team — fundamentally change their relationship to their wealth. As they transform their understanding of what their wealth can do, they also transform their vision of who they are as a family. Instead of their wealth being used only for their personal benefit, it becomes a creative tool for political, economic, cultural, and social improvement. Their money had always made them different *from* others, but now their united purpose enables them to use the money to make a difference *for* others. In cases where the money had become a burden, Lee's Unique Process turns it into a blessing.

In order to understand how and why The Quadrant Living Experience transforms both wealthy families and the societies in which they live, let's look at the underlying principles of Lee's process and relate them to The Advisor Century.

- **Wealthy families multiplying:** In 2006, the number of families in the U.S. with annual incomes over $10 million exceeded 10,000. Many of them are directly involved in the industries that are advancing the power of the microchip, or are in those industries, such as investments, that are directly benefitting from the microchip revolution. The economist Paul Zane Pilzer has a formula to describe the exponential growth that the microchip enables: $W = R \times T$. Wealth equals resources times technology. Wherever people are working, the microchip makes all their activities more productive. Wherever people are communicating, the microchip makes all their interactions easier, faster, and cheaper. Wherever people in all sectors of society are experimenting and innovating, microchip-based tools make their efforts more practical and profitable.

Extraordinary prediction. The mutual fund pioneer, Sir John Templeton, made an extraordinary prediction the same day that the stock market collapsed on October 1987. The Dow Jones Industrial Average had dropped almost 40 percent to 1,700 before trading was suspended. "Sir John," a reporter asked, "what do you think this indicates for the future of the stock market?" Templeton responded, "I think that by the year 2000, the Dow will be at 10,000." After one of the worst days in stock market history, he was predicting an almost 600 percent increase over just the next 13 years. The reporter was dumbfounded. He asked Sir John how he could possibly make that prediction. Templeton replied, "Because, of all the scientists, engineers, technicians, and inventors who have ever lived, 99 percent of them are alive today, and they are all interconnected electronically. How can there not be just an unlimited number of new things to invest in?" This is precisely what has happened over the past two decades, just as Sir John predicted.

Because of the microchip revolution, more and more individuals and families will become wealthy in ways that would have been incomprehensible 50 years ago. The needs and the impact of these families will become a major economic, political, cultural, and social theme as we go forward. At no time in history was it ever necessary to have formal training and education programs for wealthy families, because so few human beings ever experienced this condition. During the 21st century, hundreds of millions of individuals will be members of the kinds of wealthy families that can benefit from Lee Brower's Quadrant Living Experience. For that reason, the educational template Lee has created makes an enormous contribution to the health and dynamism of our "affluent society."

- **The "four quadrant" model:** When Lee began working with wealthy families, especially those whose fortunes had lasted several generations, he noticed a pattern: *In almost every case, the family's wealth had been generated from the imagination, risk-taking, and hard work of an entrepreneur — or someone collaborating with an entrepreneur.*

These individuals possessed three different kinds of capital: First, the core assets or *human capital* of being an outstanding entrepreneur and businessperson. Second, the experience assets or *intellectual capital* — the ideas and innovations — that gave rise to the fortune and legacy. And, third, the *financial capital* that was the product of the first two kinds of capital. In addition, the originating wealth creator usually created large amounts of contribution assets or *civic capital* by creating jobs, providing increased tax revenues, and through large amounts of charitable and philanthropic giving. Virtually every community in the United States, especially, is filled with the handiwork of wealthy benefactors — almost always entrepreneurs — who contributed significantly to the progress of everyone living there. This is true in many other advanced capitalist countries, as well.

Only one kind of capital left. What Lee discovered from observing how wealth had passed through several generations was that usually only one kind of capital — *financial* — was still present in many families. The human capital was no longer there. The outstanding qualities of the original entrepreneur had declined or disappeared. No new intellectual capital was now being created by the family members. And, in many cases, family life was now about the money, and very little else. There was little contribution to the civic environment surrounding the family. Even if money was being given to charity, there was no creative, purposeful, and dynamic leadership coming from family members in the outside community. What Lee Brower surmised from this trend was that the family was having difficulties with their financial capital precisely because they had lost touch with the other three forms of capital. They couldn't solve their fundamental family issues by simply looking at the money. They had to restore a comprehensive understanding of what their entire family legacy was truly about — and then make it whole, complete, and dynamic in the future.

When they brought the other three forms of capital — core, experience, and contribution — back into their discussions, thinking, decision-making, and activities, the damage caused by money could be repaired.

- **Integration and focus:** One of the things that became clear to Lee was that the members of wealthy families don't want their lives to be about money. But because of the way traditional estate planning works in America, they are constantly forced into a singular focus on financial assets. As Lee puts it, "Traditional estate planning operates around the four

D's: *divide* the assets, *defer* those assets downstream as far as possible, then *dump* them on what are, most times, the ill prepared heirs, and watch those assets *dissipate.*" Even with the best will in the world, most families will come to misunderstanding and conflict as a result of such planning. Inside Lee's four quadrant system — officially known as The Brower Quadrant[†] — all the individual family members see that their best future lies in greater cooperation, creativity, and contribution. The incentive moves away from selfishness and greed toward the integration of ambitions and a focus on "family impact" in the world.

Six stages. Lee's Quadrant Living Experience[†] involves six stages that everyone in the family goes through.

1. The Location And Vision Experience[†]. The first stage is an assessment of where the family is, and where they want to go as a unified team. This involves looking at the assets and liabilities in each of the four quadrants. Lee says that when family members are asked to put the four kinds of capital in order of priority, financial always comes out last.

2. The Empowered Wealth Solution[†]. The second stage involves creating an overall plan with strategies for improving the capital in each quadrant.

3. The Empowered Wealth Design Team[†]. The third stage involves a team of "empowered wealth" specialists and experts — from law, accounting, philanthropy, and psychology — who can execute and implement the game-plan in all areas.

4. The Solution Empowerment[†]. The design team creates a blueprint, which the family approves. This plan contains strategies for maximizing the family's assets on an ongoing basis. At this point, in the fourth stage, all of the actual implementation begins.

5. The Empowered Family Retreat[†]. When all the strategies of the initial plan have been implemented, the family meets to review everything that has been achieved. This fifth stage is facilitated by Lee, his team members, and specialists from the design team.

6. The Perpetual Confidence Builder†. The sixth stage is continual development and expansion of the family's overall Quadrant Living game-plan. One of the key tools used in this process is called The Family Empowered Co-operative†, which represents a comprehensive family governance system. Lee says that this organizational structure truly makes the family proactive with its wealth. The family members continually become more confident about the unique advantages and opportunities that their four quadrants give them.

- **Rejuvenated capital:** The Brower Quadrant approach in Lee Brower's process not only integrates the activities, values, and goals of wealthy families, it also rejuvenates their capital. Invariably, they make far better use of financial assets, so that these start growing where they had been depleted. The brainpower and intellectual capital of the family is maximized within collective goal-setting. All of the family members begin communicating and acting according to their highest ideals and biggest goals. This brings out, enhances, and focuses the human capital that has been diffused and neglected. And the family now plays an active role in making their outside communities more successful and vibrant.

- **Counteracting anti-wealth:** Wealth, in general, and wealthy families, in particular, have been the target of ideological enemies for the past two centuries. The dynamic impact and success of industrial capitalism in the early 19th century gave rise to critics who saw it as an evil force in society. At the same time, the wealth-creating powers of capitalism raised the standard of whole populations — although not in equal ways. Starting in the 1850s, anti-capitalist political movements worked to gain political control over the distribution of wealth in all industrial societies. Wealthy people were branded as parasites living off the labor of the masses. Wealthy families were described as the breeding ground for arrogance and selfishness in society. This anti-wealth ideology resulted in various forms of institutional socialism and communism that became influential throughout the 20th century. The microchip, of course, made all of these governments increasingly untenable. Not only has wealth-creation survived its worst enemies, but our opportunities for creating new wealth have multiplied beyond all reckoning. Still, those who loathe the existence of wealthy individuals and families are always hard at work to stir up public envy and resentment.

Lee Brower feels that The Quadrant Living Experience counteracts these attempts to label wealthy families as parasites. There is no question that capitalism produces inequality among individuals and families. This has always been the case, and always will be. *The only question is whether this inequality is a destructive or creative factor in society.*

Estate planning is a culprit. Lee believes that the traditional form of estate planning that has been advocated by financial services companies always places wealthy families in the worst possible light. The public spectacle of wealthy families tearing themselves apart in long, drawn-out battles over money gives ammunition to those who hate them. The individual selfishness, mindless consumption, and wasted lives that so often accompany multi-generational wealth increase the pressure to redistribute wealth through political means. They also give rise to anti-wealth policies and programs that not only punish those who have inherited wealth, but make it increasingly difficult for entrepreneurs to create it.

The wealthy as role models. Lee Brower believes that we have entered a new era where wealth can be put into a permanently positive light. When increasing numbers of wealthy families become positive role models for millions of aspiring families, all of society benefits. When the four quadrants of capital can be maximized for the benefit of the community, wealthy people will be seen as far greater contributors to the general good than their critics and enemies.

- **Educational template:** Over the past decade, Lee Brower has been contacted by hundreds of financial advisors to learn about his system. He has created a coaching program that enables these individuals to license The Quadrant Living Experience and its components. Clearly, the good word about his work, impact, and results has spread quickly through networks of wealthy families across the country. His personal work schedule is filled a year ahead, along with those of his team and colleagues. Lee is in demand as a featured speaker in financial advisor forums throughout the industry. But perhaps the most intriguing inquiries have come from presidents and boards members of colleges and universities. Leaders in post-secondary education across the country are recognizing that colleges and universities must be about more than narrow career training, as has increasingly been the trend over the past 50 years. What these educators are recognizing is that the purpose of their institutions should be the education of "high impact humans" — men and women who make a positive difference in all areas of society. The Quadrant Living Experience seems custom-made as a high-impact curriculum to achieve what these educators envision. Work is presently underway with several colleges and universities to have four-quadrant curricula available not only for their students, but also for their alumni.

Reaching millions.

Lee Brower represents one side of the spectrum. He makes an enormous social contribution by helping wealthy families become more productive stewards of their resources. Wealthy families have always had an oversized influence on society. Because they have so many resources at their disposal, their impact is always magnified. If the 10,000 wealthiest families in the United States can become more confident about the purpose of money in their lives, the results in areas like philanthropy will be just extraordinary. Thousands of communities and social causes will benefit from this "empowered wealth."

On the other side of the spectrum, however, important opportunities exist for advisors who can help the 99 percent who are not yet millionaires. The major challenge here is a lack of financial literacy. Because people are being given more responsibilities to take control of their financial future and make financial decisions, it's crucial that they have the knowledge to make sound decisions. But too many people are essentially financially illiterate; they don't have the knowledge or personal habits to make sound financial decisions. People who are financially illiterate are much less likely to become productive members of society. Crime, drug-use, and broken families are all by-products of financial illiteracy.

We've already talked about David Bach, who has made an enormous impact in this area. David's bestselling books have helped millions of people improve their financial literacy and adopt better financial habits. As David says, "Forty percent of baby boomers have nothing in savings, and the average American has about $1,000 liquid. Seventy percent of the people we surveyed are living paycheque to paycheque. I think the world would be a much better place if more of us could have the time and freedom to focus on our Unique Abilities, but too many people are unable to do this because they're living paycheque to paycheque. So hopefully my books can help alleviate some of these social ills by improving the nation's financial literacy."

Another related social challenge comes from the issue of retirement security. As the baby boomers age, millions of people can no longer rely on generous pension plans and other corporate safety nets. Meanwhile, the government has continually struggled to guarantee the long-term solvency of programs like social security. Financial advisors can make a valuable social contribution by helping people take control of their retirement security.

For example, Strategic Coach client Charlie Epstein has worked hard to address this issue. Not only has Charlie created a highly profitable Unique Process, The 401k Coach[†††], but he has enabled thousands of other advisors to transform their entire approach to the marketing and implementation of 401k plans. Because of his efforts, these advisors are now doing a far better job implementing 401k's for their clients, who in turn are enjoying much greater retirement security.

Millions of baby boomers are ready for support in this area. Whenever Charlie travels, he wears a 401k Coach t-shirt. People constantly come up to him and say, "I could really use a 401k coach." On airplanes, flight attendants are continually asking Charlie, "Could you help me with my 401k?"

When it comes to addressing the social challenges of retirement security, Charlie has a clear vision: "Let's do it in a creative way. Let's do it in an entertaining, informative, and educational way. The system is already in place to solve the problem in the private marketplace — just free the advisor's hand. That's my message to the government. And we think The 401k Coach Program[†††] is in a great position to help advisors understand this climate, and capture this opportunity."

Expanded role for advisors. Everything that has been described in this chapter points to the elevated role of financial advisors in the years ahead. In The Strategic Coach, we have hundreds of financial advisors who have created Unique Processes to deal with various aspects of The Great Crossover. You have already met a few: Dan Taylor focuses on the cooperation between adult children and their aging parents; Mary Anne Ehlert focuses on families with individuals with special needs; Charlie Epstein focuses on the transformed use of 401k plans to handle the pension and retirement needs of the entire salaried population; Chuck Brewster focuses on how cash flow can be used to create security and wealth; Scott Keffer focuses on how charities and donors can cooperate to produce major social and cultural improvements in every community; and David Bach focuses on how vast numbers of people can begin developing better financial habits. Several other industry-transforming Unique Process Advisors have been profiled in our *Creative Destruction* subscription series, including Betty Norman, Debra Franklin-Schatzki, Tom Miller, Rob Darnbrough, and Mike Campbell.

All of these advisors are making an enormous social contribution, and continually demonstrating the extraordinary potential of their profession. And this potential has only recently been unleashed. Things will only get more exciting from here. In the decades to come, Unique Process Advisors will continually help millions of people make the transition to economic adulthood and live fuller, more enriching lives.

The great split. As we suggested earlier, the financial services industry will increasingly split into two realms: the global commoditizers and the Unique Process Advisors. Every week, I get new evidence from the field that this split is occurring at an accelerated rate. Financial corporations will become larger, fewer, and more global. Unique Process Advisors will become more numerous, varied, useful, and influential. Between these two extremes lie a number of bureaucratic organizations that will disappear, and a number of commodity-based advisors who will find life increasingly difficult. But neither global commoditizers nor entrepreneurial advisors are the key players in the growth of the financial services industry. The most important force for change will be the never-ending demand for greater choice and freedom on the part of billions of consumers.

Throughout this book, we have tried to make this point vivid. Wherever people desire increased choice and freedom, Unique Process Advisors will be developing innovative methods and solutions. And for that reason, we are firmly convinced that The Advisor Century will be the most exciting century in human history.

4.

Gameplan:
From Commoditization
To Unique Process

Part 4

The
Advisor
Century

Gameplan:
From Commoditization To Unique Process

Throughout this book, I have tried to map the territory that financial advisors will travel during the 21st century. In this final chapter, I am going to lay out a practical gameplan through which advisors can achieve the freedom and monetary rewards that many Unique Process Advisors are already enjoying. Before doing this, however, I would like to provide some context.

From misfits to global change-agents.
I have been working with financial advisors since 1974. One thing I've noticed about many advisors is that they tend to be "misfits." By this, I mean that none of them set out early in life to be financial advisors. When they were growing up and going through school, they never had a career goal or dream that led them to their present role. For the most part, they are individuals who do not fit comfortably into organizational structures. Many of them do not like regular routines and regimens that have been created by other people. They don't like taking orders from people who can't sell or who have never solved problems for an actual consumer.

In my work with over 6,000 advisors, I have never found two advisors who approach the marketplace in the same way. Each of them has developed unique problem-solving capabilities. For that reason, they often do not view other financial advisors as competitors. Instead, they know that their entire success lies in the power and depth of their unique relationships with clients; no other advisor can develop the same connections in the same ways.

I believe that this "misfit" quality is one of the greatest strengths of the profession. Because most advisors never planned to be in the financial services industry, they don't have any particular investment in, or allegiance to, its institutional structures or habits. Whenever they are provided with a bypass that lessens their dependency on bureaucracy and shields them from regulation, they jump at it. This is why they will be so eager to embrace the Unique Process approach that we have advocated throughout the book.

Origins of the idea.

I first began to identify the potential of Unique Process Advisors through my experiences with a British client in 1992. At that time, the insurance industry in the U.K. mandated full disclosure of agent commissions. When an insurance policy was sold, the policyholder received a letter from the company specifying how much commission the agent had earned on the sale. My client, upon hearing this news, decided to change his entire approach to the marketplace: "I decided there was no way any client of mine was ever going to receive one of those disclosure letters."

In response, he approached the three companies that provided him with products and asked them to strip all commissions out of the policies he sold through them. He would provide the insurance to clients at wholesale prices. When the executives of one company asked him how he was going to make a living, he replied, "That's my problem, not yours. Just give me good products."

What he did with each of his clients was establish an annual "insurance management program," which consisted of frequent meetings throughout the year to make sure everything was always up to date. He charged an annual renewable fee for this program, which he found the clients were happy to pay. What surprised him the most was how much more valuable he had become to clients: "They now see me as their central financial and business advisor in ways that were never true when I was receiving commissions. My understanding of business, finance, taxation, succession planning, and a whole host of other subjects has increased enormously. The advice I can now confidently give goes far beyond life insurance. The solutions I can provide far exceed life insurance products."

Sure enough, since the early 90s, this advisor's financial business has expanded to include all of Europe. He now operates in many different countries with clients whose interests and activities are global in nature and scope.

What I realized from analyzing this British advisor's strategy was that the breakthrough occurred when he freed himself from his dependency on commissions. I began to grasp that advisors needed to develop strategies for attaining a separate, independent income stream.

Fast-forward a few years. In 1999, I had another conversation with a very successful advisor who had been in The Strategic Coach Program for five years. Unlike the British advisor, he was still dependent on commissions. I asked him, "What are you going to do when they eliminate all of your commissions?" He responded that "they," the financial corporations, weren't going to do that. I responded that they won't do it in one fell swoop, but with each passing year, they will make it more difficult for you to do business and get paid. I told him, "There's going to come a time in a couple of years when you decide that the frustrations are so great, it's not worth being in the business any more. You'll quit, which is the same thing as having your commissions eliminated."

So successful, no licenses needed. This conversation had a big impact on him. He immediately set out to create his own Unique Process and freed himself from product-based compensation. Since then, he has become so successful with not just one process, but three, that he has actually given up all of his licenses. He no longer directly receives product-based commissions or fees, and he makes far more money now than he did during his best product sales year. He has organized his company in such a way that commissions and fees are paid to licensed colleagues. As the owner of the company, he still benefits from these sales through shareholder dividends, but his Unique Process income far exceeds his product-based income. This client's example has been followed and repeated by other advisors in The Strategic Coach Program, and their successes are giving more advisors the confidence to move in a similar direction.

Different paths to the same place.

I tell these stories to illustrate the process through which two advisors came to the career-changing realization that they needed to overcome their dependency on commissions. Once they arrived at this crucial insight, everything else was set in motion. Yet thousands of advisors have yet to experience this "awakening." Our purpose in this book has been to help many advisors grasp, perhaps for the first time, the extraordinary path that is in front of them. But we want to be clear about one point: No two advisors will experience this path in exactly the same way. For some advisors, things will happen rapidly. They have become so dissatisfied with their place in the industry that they are ready to do whatever it takes to acquire independence. Other advisors may experience a more gradual transition that unfolds over several years.

Advisors will also differ in the degree to which they retain organizational commitments. Take, for example, the issue of industry licenses. I just gave you the example of an advisor who has relinquished all of his industry licenses and experienced great success in doing so. This advisor simply came to a determination that the hassles associated with these licenses far outweighed the benefits. But this was an entirely personal judgement, and we recognize that this approach may not be appropriate for other advisors. In The Strategic Coach Program, for example, we have many Unique Process Advisors, including people featured in this book, who have made the conscious decision to retain their industry licenses. Still, we think it's important to emphasize that no advisor should feel chained or paralyzed by his licenses. There is nothing at all that makes these licenses a requirement for operating as a successful Unique Process Advisor. *You are in control of your licenses; they don't control you.*

Five stages, twenty steps. With these caveats in mind, we want to close this book by outlining a path to freedom that has been pioneered within The Strategic Coach Program. This path is presented in the form of a five-stage, 20-step gameplan that describes how advisors can create a much more satisfying future.

Stage 1: Awareness.

Personal improvement always starts with increased awareness of the present situation. For many financial advisors, the overwhelming desire for financial survival and security has made them unaware of the threats to their career and livelihood. The following are four "awareness" steps that will enable advisors concerned about their future to wake up to the growing set of dangers that is gradually depriving them of capability, opportunity, and income.

1. Develop and nurture a creative anger that hostile lawyers are interfering with your future value creation and success. The combination of tort lawyers in the marketplace, regulatory lawyers at the industry level, and compliance lawyers in financial companies, creates an increasingly hostile environment for innovative financial advisors. Not one of these lawyers has the least interest in creating value for your clients — but they have both the capability and the intent to undermine your career — and this should make you mad: mad enough to create a new kind of value creation company that permanently bypasses a lawyer-controlled industry.

2. Recognize that most of your current frustrations and future problems as an advisor are caused by your industry licenses. The reason lawyers have control over you is that you have one or several licenses to sell financial commodities. Right now, your income probably depends on having those licenses — but every new frustration you face over the coming years will be a result of your increasing exposure to legal restrictions and coercion. If you were to create a new way to earn income within your client relationships that did not require a license, you would be able to escape much of the annoyance, frustration, and anxiety you are currently experiencing.

3. Recognize that bureaucratic executives and managers in financial services companies don't care about your clients — and never will. Financial companies are filled with executives and managers whose jobs are as commoditized — and as uncertain — as the products they produce. Your clients and your relationships with your clients will never be a priority in their planning and policies. This situation will not get better; it will only get worse in the years ahead. You will need to base your relationships with your clients on an innovative, evolving foundation where you can continually increase your value creation — remaining completely immune to head office uncertainties and turmoil.

4. Recognize that being dependent on commoditized products increasingly undermines your success, satisfaction, and significance. Right now, you probably still need to be selling commoditized products that require your industry licenses. But remember, over the long run, another strategy is needed — one that frees you from commoditization, regulation, and bureaucracy. It may not be completely clear to you how this can be done, but take confidence from the fact that hundreds (soon to be thousands) of other advisors like you are already enjoying the kind of creative freedom that you want for yourself. This freedom can also be yours.

Stage 2: Preparation.

Once licensed advisors become aware of the growing threats to their future success, they begin taking steps to create an escape route from the regulated industry. This requires that they organize their thinking, communications, and actions in a completely "non-industry" way. Since the industry operates entirely from a commodity sales point of view, the alternative is to see everything from the standpoint of creating new kinds of value for clients. This requires taking the following four significant steps:

5. See yourself, first and foremost, as an entrepreneur — with a specialty in financial knowledge, tools, and solutions. In order to escape from a commoditized industry, it's necessary to look at things from an entrepreneurial viewpoint. You've already proven that you know how to create opportunities in the marketplace based on your ability to listen and solve problems. This means that you are truly an entrepreneur. From this point forward, see yourself entirely as an entrepreneur at the center of a growing entrepreneurial business. Right now, it is your specialty in financial products and services that gives you your entrepreneurial opportunities. But in the future, your entrepreneurial opportunities will come from your ability to develop value creation relationships that don't depend on commodities.

6. Identify the specific reasons why your five best clients value their ongoing relationship with you and your team. Your five best clients — either past or present — have already provided you with all the clues to indicate what your entrepreneurial future will look like. Analyze why these clients value you. Is it because of your commoditized products? Not likely. Your commoditized services? Probably not. The value lies someplace else, and always will. The truth is that they see you as an extremely valuable advisor and confidant because you help them see their future and think about it clearly and confidently, in a way that no one else can do. The commodities you sell are the least valuable thing they receive from you.

7. Identify all the key issues of your clientele that can't be addressed or solved with financial commodities. Analyze all the different issues that your five best clients have: their dangers, where they are in danger of losing something; their opportunities, where they have the possibility of gaining something of value; and their strengths, where they already have existing capabilities, resources, and advantages that can be better utilized. Once you've completed this D.O.S. analysis, you'll notice that clients have many different issues and needs that financial companies completely ignore because their products provide no solutions. This universe of D.O.S. issues is where your unlimited opportunity to create value lies.

8. Master The D.O.S. Conversation as quickly as possible and use it as the basis of all client relationships. In The Strategic Coach Program, we have taught thousands of financial advisors how to build their relationships with clients around The D.O.S. Conversation. To spread this wisdom, we have created a special package consisting of a textbook and audio CDs, that shows you how to conduct this conversation. It takes only a few weeks to make this a comfortable and confident approach to all client situations. The results are always extraordinary and gratifying. By mastering The D.O.S. Conversation as quickly as possible, you will also see clearly how you can escape from relying on commoditized product sales for your future income.

Stage 3: Escape.

Regulators and bureaucratic executives and managers in the financial services industry much prefer that you see yourself as an isolated individual dealing with them directly. This is their strategy to keep you trapped. Your best escape strategy is to surround yourself with different kinds of supportive and protective communities. Here are the four steps that will enable you to escape from an industry that wants to keep you trapped:

9. Become a lifetime member of The Strategic Coach community of entrepreneurs who are transforming many different industries.

Over the past 30 years, The Strategic Coach Program has evolved as a unique global community for entrepreneurs in 60 different industries, from a dozen different countries, who desire a constant increase in creative freedom in all areas of their personal and business lives. Among the thousands of Program participants are many financial advisors who are declaring their independence from their commoditized industry. Once you join The Strategic Coach, you will immediately have a growing base of entrepreneurial support, inspiration, and learning that enables you to cut off all dependencies on bureaucratic and regulatory structures. With each passing quarter as a participant in The Strategic Coach Program, the importance and relevance of the commoditized industry will fade in your mind. [For more information on The Strategic Coach Program, see page 235.]

10. Focus on your Unique Ability and build a continually expanding Unique Ability® Team around everything you do. You have a Unique Ability that comes out most when you are creating and providing solutions for your clients. This Unique Ability has four characteristics: First, it's a superior skill that others recognize and appreciate; second, you love this activity — you can't get enough of it; third, it's always energizing for you and others around you; and, fourth, you keep getting better at it — you'll never stop improving for as long as you are doing it. It is this Unique Ability that will replace commoditized products as the source of your future income. The first step is to identify your Unique Ability. The next step is to continually build a Unique Ability Team that consists of other individuals who are skilled at and passionate about all the activities that you are not. [The book, *Unique*

Ability®: Creating The Life You Want offers more guidance on how to identify and focus your Unique Ability. See Further Reading for details.]

11. Build a Master D.O.S. Platform™ that encompasses and communicates all of your value creation strategies. With your Unique Ability identified, and having mastered The D.O.S. Conversation, you are now in a position to create The D.O.S. Platform™ that serves as your foundation for all client relationships. This platform increasingly deepens and expands the value creation possibilities that your clients will see from working with you. Once they see The D.O.S. Platform, they will immediately differentiate you from all their other advisors — and give you opportunities to help them that are not available to anyone else.

12. Transform all of your value creation activities into a Unique Process that clients pay for separately — regardless of any product sales. The use of The D.O.S. Platform with your clientele automatically leads to a Unique Process of thinking, decision making, and action that is not possible under any other circumstances. The kinds of results that clients achieve within a Unique Process are so extraordinary that they want to pay — separately and up front — to participate in it. Once they begin deriving benefits from the Unique Process, clients want this to be the basis for an ongoing relationship. The value to clients of their involvement in the Unique Process is so great and so significant that you automatically become their most trusted advisor. None of this, in any way, depends on any commoditized product.

Stage 4: Freedom.
The creation and use of a Unique Process by financial advisors immediately and automatically frees them from the regulatory and bureaucratic constraints of the financial services industry. A Unique Process Advisor enjoys a freedom of thinking, decision making, and action that would be inconceivable for the many other advisors who are dependent upon life insurance companies, investment banks, and most broker dealer organizations. Once Unique Process Advisors gain their freedom, their entrepreneurial progress can accelerate quickly through the following steps:

13. Develop and continually expand a high-quality Unique Process client base. Satisfied Unique Process clients quickly spread the good news to others like them. You find that the vast majority of the best clients in the marketplace dislike being approached by financial advisors selling commodities, while they jump at the opportunity to look at their futures through the creative structures of your Unique Process. Since you are increasingly operating outside of regulatory controls, there is no limit to the value you can create to address your clients' evolving issues. This ability becomes central to your unique positioning in the marketplace.

14. Increase your Unique Process income so that it surpasses your income from commodities. As your value creation increases, so does the price of your Unique Process. There is no upper limit to how much you can make by developing and expanding this process. Very quickly, you reach the point where your Unique Process income matches and then exceeds the amount of money you receive from commodity sales. At this point, the last remaining hold the bureaucratic industry has on your future is quickly disappearing.

15. Hire and train specialists to expand your Unique Process — and other licensed advisors to handle product sales. The organization that forms around a Unique Process is far superior to one that focuses on commodity sales. For one thing, it is much easier to attract and utilize talented people within a Unique Process™ Company. Everyone understands how value is created and how value creation can continually be increased. At the same time, commodity products are used only in the implementation of certain strategies within the Unique Process. This makes it possible to have other licensed advisors within your organization handle the sale and implementation of these products. Over time, as more clients enter the Unique Process, the importance of the commodity products, both strategically and economically, decreases.

16. Separate your Unique Process Company from your regulated product company — or perhaps eliminate your licenses altogether. The continued growth of your Unique Process Company enables you to minimize the importance of your regulated product company. Now it's time to separate these into two legal entities, so that nothing that happens on the commodity side can impact the development and expansion of your Unique Process. Depending on how you want to develop your Unique Process Company, you may decide to eliminate your personal licenses altogether. A growing number of Unique Process Advisors are creating strategic alliances with other advisors who still retain their licenses. These licensed advisors handle all of the advisory and implementation activities related to investments and insurance. The main point here is that this is your choice, and you have this choice because you are operating as a true entrepreneur rather than as a seller of commodities.

Stage 5: Significance.

As you become more independent within your Unique Process Company, you also become more useful in the marketplace and within society. Not only are you creating entirely new kinds of value for your clients, you are also innovating new solutions to larger issues in society. Your unique career background, which combines psychological insight with a mastery of financial tools, enables you to address societal dangers and opportunities in a way that is impossible for other specialists or professionals. These last four steps will take you from a Unique Process Company to an Intellectual Capital Company, creating unique value in an ever expanding arena:

17. Transform your Unique Process Company into an "Intellectual Capital Company." Your Unique Process represents your own intellectual property. I say this to differentiate it from the commodity products you have been selling that are the intellectual property of the financial corporations that designed, developed, and packaged them. It's very important that you use intellectual property lawyers to protect your creation as soon as possible. This protection can take the form of patents, trademarks, copyrights, trade secrets, trade dress, and trade design.

As you develop these protections and continue to market your Unique Process successfully, your business will turn into what we call an "Intellectual Capital Company." The term intellectual capital means that you are now getting paid for your own brainpower, wisdom, and creativity. The future of your company is now based on the development and expansion of your Unique Process. Inside of the process, you will continually be creating new concepts, tools, and systems that you — and other advisors — can use to solve important problems. As your Unique Process evolves, many of your value creation activities will have a usefulness that goes beyond your own client base. Many other individuals — including other financial advisors — will become customers who purchase your intellectual capital in one way or another. At this point, your entrepreneurial venture can become an Intellectual Capital Company that utilizes the financial services marketplace as one of its distribution channels.

18. Position your Intellectual Capital Company as a monopoly within a "value creation niche" that resists all competition and regulation. The vast majority of financial advisors are commodity sellers who lack a Unique Process. It is only by having a Unique Process that an advisor can develop an Intellectual Capital Company that provides concepts and tools that are increasingly useful within the industry. As this Intellectual Capital Company becomes well known for creating extraordinary value, it also becomes a monopoly within a particular market niche. This monopoly position makes the Unique Process Advisor immune to all forms of commoditization and competition.

19. Continually develop new value creation solutions that bypass and make obsolete bureaucratic organizations and their products. An Intellectual Capital Company that continually innovates new value creation concepts, tools, and systems represents a great threat to bureaucratic organizations in the industry. There is nothing bureaucratic executives and managers can do to compete with new value offerings in the marketplace that bypass commoditized products. As more Unique Processes become Intellectual Capital Companies, the turmoil, confusion, and disintegration within bureaucratic structures accelerate. This creates even more entrepreneurial opportunities for the development and expansion of your Unique Process organization.

20. Enter into value creation alliances with other innovative

advisors who operate their own Intellectual Capital Companies. Within the next ten years, there will be thousands of Intellectual Capital Companies operating throughout the financial services industry — all of them bypassing the comprehension and controls of bureaucratic and regulatory organizations. In essence, there will now be a global culture of entrepreneurial advisors who feed off one another's innovation and growth. By creating strategic alliances with other Intellectual Capital Companies within this global culture, you will open yourself up to endless opportunities for increased capabilities, resources, and success.

Embracing The Advisor Century.

Over the past 30 years, I have discovered that there are two types of financial advisors: those who want the security of a large corporation backing them up, and those who continually strive for greater personal and professional freedom. Obviously, the 20-step path I have just described is only for the latter. It's for those individuals who became financial advisors so that they could operate as entrepreneurs. Huge portions of the industry are presently geared against them — but we are totally supportive of them. The path that we have laid out here is not a theory. It reflects the actual steps that hundreds of Unique Process Advisors have taken to transform their futures.

As this book concludes, one point should be very clear: The Advisor Century has arrived, and there is nothing that politicians, corporate executives, or lawyers can do about it. The bureaucratic forces in our world will continually put up obstacles and roadblocks, but these obstacles will always be overcome by the enormous ingenuity and capability of Unique Process Advisors. The only question is whether advisors themselves will recognize the extraordinary opportunities in front of them, and take the steps necessary to enter The Advisor Century. I began this book with a simple but provocative statement: Never has there been a more exciting time to be a financial advisor. Hopefully, after reading this book, you have come to understand why.

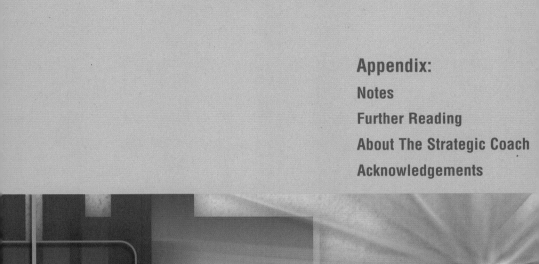

Appendix:
Notes

Further Reading

About The Strategic Coach

Acknowledgements

The
Advisor
Century

Notes

1. Joseph Schumpeter (1883-1950) was an Austrian economist whose insights and observations about entrepreneurialism, especially its role in what he called the "creative destruction" of the capitalist system, are enjoying a renaissance among politicians and economists around the world. In his most famous work, *Capitalism, Socialism and Democracy* (1942), Schumpeter warns that modern corporations, and the political-economic society that grows around them, will produce increasingly influential elite intellectual and bureaucratic classes that are enemies of both capitalism and entrepreneurs.

2. Cited in William Whyte, *The Organization Man* (Garden City, New York: Doubleday, 1956) p. 3. The imagery of a "man in a gray flannel suit" is often attributed most prominently to Sloan Wilson, who had an influential book by that name.

3. This contention that living standards in western countries are better than ever is controversial. Not surprisingly, it is frequently contested by doom and gloom pundits who argue that inflation-adjusted incomes have stagnated and inequality has increased. This debate is currently playing out among economists. Without getting into a war of statistics, we should make several important points.

   First, we acknowledge that significant income inequality remains in countries like the United States. Indeed, our central argument is that the microchip revolution accelerates the inequality between those who can utilize this technology to increase their capabilities, and those who remain stuck in a state of economic dependency. However, because this inequality is being created by the innovative efforts of entrepreneurs, it represents a form of "creative inequality." And some degree of creative inequality is always healthy. That doesn't mean we should simply ignore the plight of the poor. But the best way to improve their situation is by empowering them to become more "Microchip Friendly" in all areas of their lives. Financial advisors such as David Bach and Doug Andrew, who we profile in the Usefulness section of this book, have already helped millions of people improve their financial literacy and take control over their financial futures.

Nonetheless, we want to suggest that, despite the presence of inequality, living standards are still increasing across western societies. The vast majority of people are becoming better off in all areas of their lives. The best argument for this is that the quality of goods people can buy is significantly better than it was even ten years ago. Because of new technologies, the same pool of resources buys a much better television, cell phone, and automobile than it ever has before — not to mention the numerous other products that are becoming more accessible due to technological innovation.

If you are more interested in this subject, a good place of reference is Gregg Easterbrook's book, *The Progress Paradox: How Life Gets Better While People Feel Worse* (Random House, 2003). Easterbrook responds to many of the standard arguments advanced by the pessimists, and forcefully argues that living standards are in fact becoming better all the time. Yet he also acknowledges that affluence and progress create their own set of anxieties. And that's a point we are also emphasizing: Financial advisors will continually be called upon to help their clients deal with the anxieties of affluence.

4. See Ulrich Beck, *Risk Society: Towards a New Modernity* (London: Sage Publications, 1992).

5. This argument is addressed further in Peter Drucker's essay, "Financial Services: Innovate or Die." The essay is found in his work, *Managing in the Next Society* (New York: St. Martin's, 2003).

6. Jacques Ellul's many important insights on this subject are found in his work, *The Technological Society* (Knopf/Vintage; 1967). Ellul's main thesis is that all of society is now inside of a single global system consisting of an infinite number of technologies. We are so immersed in this technological environment that we don't even recognize what has happened to us. Because we are all now "technological creatures," we are only able to observe and think in technological terms. Increasingly, the problems we encounter are technological in their origin, and the solutions we create to address them are technological in form. Every technological solution creates new technological problems, and so we are continually caught in a web of our own making. I think Ellul has a very useful way of looking at things. However, at the end of his logic, he is a complete pessimist, whereas I am increasingly optimistic. *My own conclusion is that "technology" is simply us.* It is simply a new dimension of human nature expressing itself in the world. Ever since humans created the first tools, we have been expanding both our capability and consciousness. *Microtechnology simply represents the best means for increased consciousness and capability that we have ever created, and we've just started on this new path.*

7. F. A. Hayek (1899-1992) was a leading thinker of the Austrian School of Economics, which advocated free market policies during the first half of the 20th century when many of the leading intellectuals and bureaucrats in the world were advocating socialist solutions for industrialized countries. In *The Fatal Conceit*, Hayek presents a manifesto on the "errors of socialism." He argues that, from its origins, socialism has been mistaken on both factual and logical grounds. These errors are responsible for the continued failure to apply socialism on any practical level. In his most famous book, *The Road to Serfdom*, Hayek contends that socialist policies and practices must always lead to governments that are increasingly totalitarian. *The more socialist a society becomes,*

the more it must attempt to control all economic activities and resort to police powers to prevent its citizens from innovating alternative approaches. According to Hayek, only democratic countries that protect private property and encourage entrepreneurs and free trade can continually increase both the freedom and quality of life of its citizens.

8. One good account of the rise of an "experience economy" is provided by B. Joseph Pine II and James H. Gilmore in their work, *The Experience Economy* (Harvard Business School Press, 1999).

9. See Hernando De Soto, *The Mystery of Capital: Why Capitalism Triumphs in the West and Fails Everywhere Else* (Basic Books, 2003).

10. See Shoshana Zuboff and James Maxmin, *The Support Economy* (Viking Penguin, 2002).

11. Kurt Friedrich Gödel (1906-1978) was an Austrian American mathematician and philosopher. He was deeply interested in the philosophy of mathematics and mathematical logic, and his seminal insights came during his work in these areas. He published his famous "incompleteness theorem" in 1931, shortly after earning his doctorate in Europe. He later migrated to the United States and spent much of his career at the Institute for Advanced Study in Princeton, NJ, where he was a friend and associate of Albert Einstein.

12. In this endnote, we want to expand on the concept of "life transformation" for those advisors who are particularly interested in the subject. We live in an age where people are turning to therapists and psychologists in record numbers, along with clergy, and various kinds of guidance counselors. Numerous professionals such as lawyers, accountants, personal trainers, nutrition experts, child care specialists, and tutors have stepped in to fill specific lifestyle needs and provide support. Yet we want to suggest that more than any other professional or specialist in the world today, financial advisors are positioned to provide the transformative support that people crave.

Psychology and mathematics. Financial advisors are in this position because of their unparalleled ability to skillfully combine the tools of both psychology and mathematics. We made this point earlier in the book and it deserves some more elaboration. Financial advisors are true "psychological geniuses." They have an extraordinary ability to get right to the heart of what matters to people. That's partly because financial discussions, more than any other kind of discussion, have a way of clarifying things for people. They have a way of getting people to prioritize and focus on what really matters in their life.

Yet advisors are also able to bring mathematics into the discussion. Mathematics is based on fixed laws, and "right" or "wrong" answers. In the careful hands of a financial advisor, mathematics provides tools for making financial calculations and projections with some degree of predictability. It allows advisors to realize, for their clients, the "miracle" of compound interest, and put the laws of exponential growth to work. It allows them to run asset allocation models and perform other forms of technical analysis that clearly demonstrate to clients how specific variables impact their financial situation. The result is a level of rigor that most therapists and psychologists can't match.

There are plenty of places in this world where people can go sit on a couch and talk. But financial advisors are always interested in acting and planning, not just talking.

Indeed, in a therapist's office, clients may conduct a far-ranging discussion about their goals. But rarely will they actually leave that office with a concrete action-plan to achieve these goals, backed up with real financial and mathematical rigor. You may talk to a therapist about your goals for the future. But while they may help you see things differently, there is very little that the therapist can do to help you acquire the financial resources needed to attain those goals. It's not their focus or area of expertise.

In this way, "transforming client futures" takes two related forms: life-planning and life-integration.

Life-planning. "Life-planning" is something that many advisors do intuitively with their clients, whether or not they have identified it as part of their value offering. Life-planning means stepping back from the minutia of everyday existence and focusing on the long-term trajectory of life, at each stage of its development. It means examining how different phases of the lifecycle relate to one another.

For centuries, philosophers have identified "life-planning" as an activity that reveals something important about human potentiality. That's because unlike most animals, humans can develop a temporal perspective on their life as it unfolds from beginning to end. They can weight short vs. long term and gain some sense of what they want to accomplish at each stage of existence. But never before in human history have people had the opportunity to pursue this activity in the company of such skilled financial advisors. All financial planning discussions are ultimately part of a larger process of life-planning.

Life-integration. In a similar way, advisors have the capability to assist clients with "life-integration." Life-integration is about developing a sense of balance and harmony in your life. Financial advisors can help people wade through their competing demands and achieve this balance. They will increasingly set themselves up as a clearinghouse or command center that coordinates all of the different "advisors" in a client's life — lawyers, accountants, psychologists, educational specialists, and others. In this sense, financial advisors will serve as the central "operating system" in a client's life. Regardless of how many professionals a client consults, everything always comes back to his or her relationship with the financial advisor. All of these professionals must operate within a structure that has been set up by the financial advisor; their job is simply to execute one aspect of a client's life-plan that the financial advisor is guiding. As a result, financial advisors will find themselves at the epicenter of everything important to their clients.

13. Jean-Baptiste Say (1762-1832) was a French economist and businessman who, along with the Scottish moral philosopher Adam Smith, advocated a radical lifting of government restrictions on trade, and an equally radical elimination of government interference with the workings of the entrepreneurial economy. Say's fundamental thesis was that *supply always creates its own demand — and that scarcity is always caused by government attempts to control and direct the marketplace.* His most famous work is *A Treatise on Political Economy*, published in 1803. Say's work was largely ignored or dismissed until recently, when free market economists began to recognize the originality of his thinking.

Further Reading

Delving deeper.

These are some of the books that have influenced our thinking on business and economics, books that we often recommend to Strategic Coach clients. They all complement the themes and arguments advanced in *The Advisor Century*.

Managing in the Next Society. Peter F. Drucker. St. Martin's; (2003). It's always worthwhile to hear what management expert Peter Drucker has to say. This book is a compilation of some of Drucker's most insightful essays produced over the last decade or so. Financial advisors should turn immediately to his essay, "Financial Services: Innovate or Die." Drucker argues that the financial services industry has essentially become a depleted industry increasingly resistant to innovation. The 1950s to 1970s saw innovations such as the Eurodollar, Eurobond, institutional investors, and the credit card. The 1980s produced universal life insurance and automated banking. Mutual funds gained new prominence, and bankers began to initiate and manage acquisitions. But Drucker argues that, since then, most new products have involved risky financial derivatives. Instead of creating new products in areas of potential, firms are increasingly relying on capital gains from their own investment accounts to drive growth.

The Technological Society. Jacques Ellul. Knopf/Vintage; (1967). Since 1980, I've read this book at least ten times. Jacques Ellul is one of those writers who is so perceptive in his observations and so accurate in his predictions that no one wants to read him. That's because he believes that the spread of technology in the world is taking all the humanity out of life. I don't personally share his pessimism, but I do believe that adapting to technological change is the number one challenge facing every individual.

The Support Economy. Shoshana Zuboff and James Maxmin. Viking Penguin; (2002). The authors' central thesis is that the fundamental aspirations and motivations of consumers in western countries, especially the United States, have shifted profoundly over the past half-century in ways and directions that corporations do not comprehend. Our analysis of the financial services industry certainly supports their claim: The biggest corporations clearly do not understand the motivations and desires of their end-users.

The Future and Its Enemies. Virginia Postrel. The Free Press; (1999). Virginia Postrel is one of the great advocates of innovation and economic progress in the United States. Her basic thesis is that modern technological societies, especially in America, have divided into two leadership groups: the dynamists and the stasists. The dynamists are those, like herself, who advocate increased freedom for individuals to innovate new solutions in all areas of human activity. The stasists are those who want to use the instrument of government to control and prevent innovation.

The Long Tail. Chris Anderson. Hyperion; (2006). Anderson describes how in every sector of human activity, the world is moving from a century-old reliance upon commoditized "hits" to the emergence of millions of highly profitable "niches." This trend works against the viability of large bureaucratic organizations that are too ignorant of emerging marketplace opportunities, and too inward-focused, to understand where competitive advantage lies.

The World is Flat: A Brief History of the Globalized World in the Twenty-First Century. Thomas L. Friedman. Farrar, Straus and Giroux; (2005). Thomas Friedman, a three-time winner of the Pulitzer Prize, is the foreign affairs columnist for *The New York Times*. In a previous book, *The Lexus and the Olive Tree*, he laid down the foundation for his current work. He was one of the first mainstream observers to focus on the global wave of commoditization that is disrupting economies, industries, companies, jobs, and communities around the world. This latest book takes that thesis further, identifying ten "flatteners" and three "convergences" that are making the entire global marketplace into a competitive playing field. These forces, Friedman contends, are already rendering large numbers of organizations and jobs in the Western world obsolete.

What Clients Love: A Field Guide to Growing Your Business. Harry Beckwith. Warner Business Books; (2003). Harry Beckwith is a wonderfully lucid and stimulating writer who has previously produced two other bestsellers that I highly recommend: *Selling The Invisible* and *The Invisible Touch*. All financial advisors should have these books — but especially *What Clients Love* — by their bedside. This latest book is full of hundreds of wonderful insights and strategies that can be used immediately.

The Wealth of Knowledge. Thomas A. Stewart. Currency; (2003). Thomas Stewart stresses that the ability to continually create new knowledge (intellectual capital) is the only ongoing sustainable competitive advantage of the 21st century. It doesn't require any stuff. It doesn't take up any space. It represents a competitive advantage that always favors new enterprises over the established ones. It always empowers entrepreneurs, while making bureaucracies obsolete. I would add that the raw material of intellectual capital — the emerging D.O.S. of billions of human beings in an integrated global marketplace — is inexhaustible. In fact, the more that individuals use this resource, the greater the supply becomes. And there are few, if any, barriers to entry, because new intellectual capital always evades and escapes regulation.

The Deviant's Advantage. Watts Wacker and Ryan Mathews. Crown Business; (2002). The authors have a simple thesis: All new ideas that the marketplace finds valuable are, by definition, deviant in the eyes and thinking of "the establishment" — in all fields of activity. Not only deviant, but threatening. The energy and potential of new ideas is measured precisely by how they deviate from the thinking of those who protect and preserve the status quo in any industry or organization. That is why in the financial services industry, there are unlimited opportunities for financial advisors to create their own deviant Unique Processes.

The Experience Economy. B. Joseph Pine II and James H. Gilmore. Harvard Business School Press; (1999). This well-known book provides an excellent account of the increasing importance of "experiences" as a form of marketplace value. The authors contrast the world of experiences to the older world of goods and services, and provide strategies for companies and entrepreneurs to orient their businesses around the packaging of unique experiences.

Blue Ocean Strategy. W. Chan Kim and Renée Mauborgne. Harvard Business School Press; (2005). In this visionary business strategy book, the authors suggest that, since the Industrial Age, many large corporations have focused all their energy on head-to-head competition with rivals. The result has often been a bloody "red ocean" with rivals fighting over a shrinking profit pool. According to the authors, these older principles of competitive strategy are not the best way to create profitable growth in the future. Rather, companies need to focus on creating "blue oceans" — an uncontested market space ripe for growth. Their vision is one of expanding, competition-free markets that innovative companies can navigate and prosper in.

Running Money. Andy Kessler. HarperCollins; (2004). In this in-your-face memoir, skilled investor Andy Kessler provides a colorful account of his experiences on Wall Street as he leaves the institutional investor world to co-manage a hedge fund.

The Progress Paradox: How Life Gets Better While People Feel Worse. Gregg Easterbrook. Random House; (2003). This book provides several important insights. First, Easterbrook cuts through all the skeptics to make a convincing case that our living standards are getting better all the time. People throughout western societies have never been better off than they are today. Yet Easterbrook also notices that many people, even the most affluent, continue to feel anxious about life. Easterbrook's advice is simple: The sooner people recognize how good things are, the sooner they can help make the world an even better place.

The Origin of Wealth. Eric D. Beinhocker. Harvard Business School Press; (2006). This book is a real tour de force by a fellow at the McKinsey Global

Institute, an economic think tank associated with their consulting company. The author provides a critical account of modern economic theory, arguing that much of what we have been taught is wrong. Instead, he strongly advances a new paradigm called "Complexity Economics." Essentially, the difference between traditional economic theory and Beinhocker's model reflects the difference between physics and biology. While traditional economic theory uses a physics-based model of closed systems, Beinhocker argues for an evolutionary model characterized by an open, adaptive system. Beinhocker makes sure to discuss some of the policy implications.of his theoretical insights.

Revolutionary Wealth. Alvin Toffler and Heidi Toffler. Knopf; (2006). This book is about how tomorrow's wealth will be created, and who will get it. When Alvin Toffler wrote his bestseller, *Future Shock,* in 1971, he was describing the early inability of Industrial Age organizations to cope with increases of global change. The majority of Fortune 500 corporations that dominated the U.S. economy the year that *Future Shock* was published no longer exist. The greatest new wealth creation in society now comes from the creative combination of the personal computer, the Internet, and the use of search engines by enterprising individuals and groups who bypass bureaucracy. So this book, *Revolutionary Wealth*, represents a useful attempt by Alvin and Heidi Toffler to forecast into the future and paint a picture of the dynamic environment for wealth creation that we are entering.

The Idea of Decline in Western History. Arthur Herman. The Free Press; (1997). In this work of intellectual history, the author traces the prevalent strains of pessimism found in so much western thought. He provides a useful context for understanding current day "doom and gloom" prognosticators.

Cowboy Capitalism. Olaf Gersemann. Cato Institute; (2004). This book is focused on revealing what the author calls "European myths" and "American reality." The author — a German reporter — compares the European economic model to the American model, and finds that many of the supposed advantages of the European model actually have little basis. Instead, the author finds that the market freedoms in America create a much more prosperous and efficient system that outperforms in every area the declining European welfare states.

The Rule of Lawyers. Walter K. Olson. St. Martin's; (2003). Throughout *The Advisor Century*, we have focused on the increasing intrusion of the legal profession into the financial services industry. In *The Rule of Lawyers,* Walter K. Olson provides a revealing account of the persuasive legalization that is threatening a wide range of industries. As Olson puts it, his aim in the book is to demonstrate how "the new litigation elite threatens America's rule of law." I highly recommend this book for financial advisors who want to learn more about the "lawsuit industry" — how it operates and why it has become so influential.

Made to Stick: Why Some Ideas Survive and Others Die. Chip Heath and Dan Heath. Random House; (2007). The authors focus on how businesses can achieve "stickiness" — the art of making something unforgettable. By asking why some ideas thrive while others die, the authors develop a series of principles that can help any entrepreneur develop winning ideas.

Small Giants. Bo Burlingham. Portfolio; (2005). This is a book about some of the most innovative, inspiring, and successful small businesses in America. Burlingham profiles 14 businesses that have become "giants" in their field, without becoming huge corporations.

The Attention Economy: Understanding the New Currency of Business. Thomas H. Davenport and John C. Beck. Harvard Business School Press; (2001). The authors argue that in today's world of information overload, the scarcest resource of all isn't time, money, ideas, or talent, but attention. The authors provide a range of strategies for understanding the psychology of attention, measuring attention, and using technology to expand or protect attention. They also explore insights from areas like the advertising industry on how to reach people in a world where attention is scarce.

Works by The Strategic Coach and its clients.
From The Strategic Coach

Creative Destruction. Dan Sullivan. This path-breaking subscription series goes in-depth on many of the themes discussed in *The Advisor Century*. The series is organized around "12 Predictions" for the future of the financial services industry. Packed with wisdom, each module in the series features a full-length interview with an Industry Transformer who is reshaping the profession. Available at *www.strategiccoach.com*.

The Laws of Lifetime Growth. Dan Sullivan and Catherine Nomura. Berrett-Koehler; (2006). This book outlines ten simple "laws" through which anyone can commit themselves to lifetime growth. Vivid real-life stories capture the experiences of people who have embraced these laws in all areas of their lives. For entrepreneurs who want to implement these laws in their organizations, an understanding of how they apply on a more individual level is essential. The best foundation for any organization striving for lifetime growth is a team in which each member understands these principles and is committed to lifetime growth on a personal and professional level. For more information on this book and on the laws, visit *www.lifetimegrowth.com*.

Unique Ability®: Creating The Life You Want. Catherine Nomura and Julia Waller, with Shannon Waller. The Strategic Coach. (2003). You have an incredible force called "Unique Ability." It's a combination of your personal talents, passions, and skills. You've always had this ability, but you may have never stopped to clearly identify it. This book contains a complete process that will help you identify your Unique Ability, and then immediately put it to work in your life.

From Our Clients
David Bach

The Automatic Millionaire. Broadway; (2003).
Start Late, Finish Rich. Broadway reprint edition; (2007).
Smart Couples Finish Rich. Broadway reprint edition; (2002).
Smart Women Finish Rich. Broadway; (2002).

These bestselling books offer David Bach's signature brand of accessible, useful, and easy-to-implement financial advice.

Dan Taylor

The Parent Care Conversation. Penguin; (2006). In this book, Dan Taylor discusses his visionary approach to parent care.

Doug Andrew

Missed Fortune 101. Warner Business Books; (2005). In this book, Doug Andrew outlines his powerful wealth maximization strategy. He exposes the flaws behind many commonly accepted principles of personal finance, and offers a range of unconventional yet common sense money-management advice.

About
The Strategic
Coach

The Strategic Coach® Program.

Dan Sullivan is known throughout the world as an innovator and visionary whose ideas have set the standard for others in the entrepreneurial coaching industry. The Strategic Coach Program, co-founded in 1989 with his wife and partner, Babs Smith, was the first coaching program exclusively for entrepreneurs, and remains the most innovative in terms of its ability to help participants make successive quantum leaps toward increasingly greater personal and professional goals.

Strategic Coach clients today not only significantly increase their income and free time, they build strong, future-focused companies that leave their competition behind. Many have set new standards in their industries and made significant contributions to their communities through the increased focus, resources, and creativity gained by participating in the Program. Because of these results in all areas of life, most participants continue year after year. They comment that, as their dreams grow, the Program grows with them.

The Strategic Coach Inc.

The Strategic Coach is an organization created by entrepreneurs, for entrepreneurs. The company operates using the same philosophy, tools, and concepts taught in The Strategic Coach Program, and has grown more than ten times in the past eight years. With over 100 entrepreneurially-minded team members and three offices — one in Toronto, one in Chicago, and one in the U.K. — the company continues to grow and enrich its offerings to an expanding, global client base. Currently, over 3,000 successful and highly motivated entrepreneurs from over 60 industries and a dozen countries attend Strategic Coach workshops on a quarterly basis.

If you would like more information about The Strategic Coach, its programs for entrepreneurs at all levels of success, or its many products for entrepreneurial thinkers, please call 416.531.7399 or 1.800.387.3206. Or visit *www.strategiccoach.com*.

Acknowledgements

We'd like to take the time to recognize and thank the many wonderful people who contributed their time and effort to the making of this book.

To our talented team of editors, Catherine Nomura, Myrna Nemirsky, Kerri Morrison, and Moya Dillon, thank you for all of the hard work and dedication you put into making *The Advisor Century* the best it could be.

To our amazing designers, Suzanne Noga, Jennifer Bhatthal, and Marilyn Luff, thank you for the creativity and inspiration you provided throughout the making of the book and for helping to express our ideas through your designs.

We'd like to thank Christine Nishino and Moragh Cameron for lending us their expertise in organizing and co-ordinating all aspects of the printing for *The Advisor Century*. And to our project manager, Paul Hamilton, thank you for all of your hard work and patience in ensuring that the creative process went smoothly and stayed on schedule.

To our Industry Transformers, we appreciate your willingness to share and your ability to inspire us with your stories, and for allowing us to share your experiences and Unique Processes with others. Thank you to Doug Andrew, David Bach, Lee Brower, Chuck Brewster, Mike Campbell, Rob Darnbrough, Mary Anne Ehlert, Charlie Epstein, Debra Franklin-Schatzki, Scott Keffer, Tom Miller, Betty Norman, and Dan Taylor.

We'd also like to thank a few other Unique Process Advisors who have shared their ongoing successes and experiences with us: John Backhouse, David Batchelor, Mark Bingham, John Cross, Gord Berger, Frank Creaghan, Peter Creaghan, Bob Gould, Darren Laverty, Marty McConnell, Joseph Janiczek, and Bruce Udell.